AMERICAN HERITAGE
ILLUSTRATED HISTORY
OF THE UNITED STATES

Fiddling and dancing on a raft made from tree trunks that still have some of their branches, these rivermen display their talent for having a good time.

FRONT COVER: *The train approaching the young, growing city of San Francisco was part of the transcontinental rail link.*
LIBRARY OF CONGRESS

FRONT ENDPIECE: *A peddler in a top hat presents his wares at an isolated farmhouse, trying to sell cloth, pans and needles from his horse-drawn cart.*
INTERNATIONAL BUSINESS MACHINES

CONTENTS PAGE: *The Wyoming, built in Philadelphia in 1857, was one of the gaudiest engines of its day, with surfaces covered in scrollwork and fancy brass.*
COVERDALE AND COLPITTS

BACK COVER: *Ralph Earl painted the portrait of General Andrew Jackson (top left); Eli Whitney's revolutionary cotton gin is operated on a plantation (top right); forced from their homelands (bottom), Eastern Indians immigrate to the west in what became known as the trail of tears.*
MEMPHIS BROOKS MUSEUM OF ART: LIBRARY OF CONGRESS, WOLLAROC MUSEUM

AMERICAN HERITAGE ILLUSTRATED HISTORY OF THE UNITED STATES

VOLUME 5

YOUNG AMERICA

BY ROBERT G. ATHEARN

Created in Association with the
Editors of AMERICAN HERITAGE

and for the updated edition
MEDIA PROJECTS INCORPORATED

CHOICE PUBLISHING, INC.
New York

Library of Congress Catalog Card Number: 87-73399
ISBN 0-945260-05-9

This 1988 edition is published and distributed by Choice Publishing, Inc., 53 Watermill Lane, Great Neck, NY 11021 by arrangement with American Heritage, a division of Forbes, Inc.

Manufactured in the United States of America

CONTENTS OF THE COMPLETE SERIES

Editor's Note to the Revised Edition
Introduction by ALLAN NEVINS
Main text by ROBERT G. ATHEARN

EACH VOLUME CONTAINS AN ENCYCLOPEDIC SECTION; MASTER INDEX IN VOLUME 18

CONTENTS OF VOLUME 5

CHAPTER 13

NATIONALISM RAMPANT

The most important result of the War of 1812 was the improvement in Anglo-American diplomatic relations. Even though each side regarded the settlement as something of a truce, both were eager to avoid a renewal of hostilities. England wanted to be free of any dangers at her back so that she might expand her great domain overseas. The Americans wanted to develop their Western domain.

The first major postwar settlement between the two nations was the Rush-Bagot agreement, ratified by the United States Senate in 1818. Proposed by President Madison in 1817, it dealt with the armed vessels that both countries had put on the Great Lakes during the war. Charles Bagot, British minister to the United States, exchanged notes with Richard Rush, the acting Secretary of State, which provided that each power should have no more than a single-gun 100-ton vessel on Lake Champlain and Lake Ontario, and two such vessels on Erie, Huron, Michigan, and Superior. The

This turbulent election day in Philadelphia in the autumn of 1815 was painted by German-born artist John Lewis Krimmel.

basic principles of the Rush-Bagot agreement remained in effect for many years and were reaffirmed by the United States and Canada in 1946.

Encouraged by this agreement, the two nations resolved other differences in the Convention of 1818. Right after the war Great Britain had maintained that our fishing privileges in Canadian waters, gained at the Treaty of 1783, were no longer in effect. The diplomats now agreed that fishing rights should be restored. Another unsettled difficulty concerned the Canadian-American border. The northern boundary of the Louisiana Purchase was still undefined, and although there seemed to be little chance that the area would soon be populated, both sovereignties were glad to settle on the 49th parallel for the part of the boundary between the Lake of the Woods in northern Minnesota and the Rocky Mountains. West of the Rockies, the border country was held in joint occupancy until the settlement of 1846.

The Convention of 1818 also took up the matter of American slaves carried off by the British during the War of 1812. Czar Alexander of Russia was asked to mediate, and by 1822 he submitted a recommendation awarding the United States $1,200,000 compensation for the slaves and for other debts that the British had incurred.

Dealings with Spain

The United States now turned to Spain to settle some long-standing territorial questions concerning the Floridas. American interest in that region dated back to the foundation of the Republic, and with the Louisiana Purchase, there was renewed interest in rounding out our holdings. East and West Florida not only plunged deep into the Caribbean, affecting sea connections with Louisiana, but they also controlled the mouths of navigable streams in the present states of Mississippi and Alabama.

At first the Americans tried to bluff the Spanish. Robert Livingston, who negotiated the Louisiana Purchase, knew perfectly well that it did not include the Floridas, but he pretended to so construe it. When Jefferson left office, he spoke of making Florida and Cuba a part of the Union. Later, in 1810, Madison made no objection when a group of American settlers in West Florida staged a revolt and proclaimed the Republic of Florida. In fact, when the settlers asked admittance to the United States, Madison extended American authority to West Florida. Naturally, the Spanish protested, but they were deeply involved in war and could do little to enforce

their objections. Nor could their British allies help, for they, too, were in a death struggle with Napoleon. International reaction to the Florida affair was summarized by the Russian czar. When the American minister tried to explain the situation to him, he merely bowed and remarked with a smile, "Everybody is getting a little bigger nowadays."

Meanwhile, American slaves escaped into Spanish territory with increasing frequency, as did Seminole Indians fleeing from federal troops. The inevitable crisis came in 1818. Andrew Jackson chased some of the Indians across the international border and then hanged two Englishmen, whom he accused of inciting them. The execution of Alexander Arbuthnot and Robert Ambrister angered the British, and along with the Spanish minister to Washington, they registered a sharp protest.

John Quincy Adams, Secretary of State, suggested to the Spanish that one solution of the difficulty was for the United States to buy the Floridas. After lengthy negotiations, Spain agreed, and on February 22, 1819, relinquished her claim to both East and West Florida. The Adams-Onis Treaty, named for the two negotiators, also defined the western boundary of the Louisiana Purchase and strengthened American claims to Oregon as the Spanish surrendered all rights in that territory. For all this the United States gave $5,000,000 and then agreed to make no claim to Texas

The Rush-Bagot agreement limited the number of American and British armed vessels on each of the Great Lakes. This one is at Fort Malden, Ontario.

as a result of the Louisiana Purchase.

With almost no military effort, America had settled some troublesome problems and made some significant changes in the size of the country. Generally, the proponents of nationalism were pleased. A few, like Henry Clay, thought the United States had not gone far enough. He had wanted Texas, too. The next few decades were to realize the wildest dreams of such land-hungry men.

Successful negotiations with England and Spain during the postwar years enhanced the American feeling of equality among nations. Suddenly the country emerged as a national entity, somewhat gawky and self-conscious but aware of its relative strength in the Western Hemisphere. Residents of the young land acquired a new, shoulder-swinging pride that probably annoyed the Europeans, but they were much too busy recovering from their recent conflict to restrain the youthful upstart.

From the standpoint of size, the United States posed no threat to any of the older countries. Its population was about 10,000,000 and not more than 600,000 square miles were settled, as compared to 3,000,000 today. The Union was a confederation of 24 loosely joined states, only two of them west of the Mississippi River, each still jealous of its own powers

Law on the frontier was most often a matter of an individual's power, but as settlements grew, courts were established. This 1849 painting shows a rural session where, obviously, the solemnity of the court is not being fully felt.

despite the currents of nationalism that were beginning to flow strongly.

After 1815, Americans were primarily concerned with domestic problems, both economic and political. They tended to turn their backs upon Europe and to look toward the undeveloped West. They rationalized their new orientation by rereading Thomas Paine's *Common Sense,* or by referring to George Washington's Farewell Address. Both men had warned that Europe and America had separate interests. Even the internationally minded Jefferson took this view in his later years. Out of this type of thinking grew the Monroe Doc-

trine, a theory of hemispheric isolation that was to polarize American foreign policy for a century.

The immediate reason for the doctrine's enunciation was the state of affairs in Europe. Spain, now weak and poor, was struggling to recover her South American colonies, lost by revolt during the era of the Napoleonic Wars. The Russians, Austrians, and French, deeply affected by postwar conservatism, wanted the Spanish colonies restored to their former owner. The British did not agree. After years of turmoil, England's economy was now expanding internationally, and she did not want to lose her new-found trade with such young Hispanic-American nations as Argentina and Venezuela. For years she had sought to enter those restricted markets, and now her Continental neighbors were about to deny her the fruits of her patience.

George Canning, England's foreign minister, looked around for support. He knew he was opposed by most of the other European powers in his wish to see the independence of the South American nations maintained. But he also knew the United States was opposed to any further European encroachments in the Western Hemisphere. Therefore, he turned to Richard Rush, the American minister at London, and suggested that the mother and daughter stand against any such invasion. Rush, in turn, sent the proposal to President Monroe, who promptly asked advice from his cabinet and from two old friends, Jefferson and Madison.

The Monroe Doctrine—by Adams

Both ex-Presidents advised Monroe to cooperate with the British, but Secretary of State John Quincy Adams was against it. He argued that the United States should stand alone. He knew Great Britain valued American friendship, particularly for commercial reasons. He was sure England would oppose France and the others, with or without cooperation from this side of the Atlantic. Resting his case upon these facts, he felt his country could safely act alone and need not

be a junior partner to England. As he said, "It would be more candid as well as more dignified, to avow our principles explicitly to Russia and to France, than to come in as a cockboat in the wake of the British man-of-war."

So the Monroe administration elected to hoist its own colors and sail the waters of international affairs independently. In his annual message in 1823, Monroe enunciated what was later known as his doctrine. Its sentiments, found scattered all through the message, warned Europe that the Hispanic-American nations were independent and no longer subject to colonization by foreign powers. He reiterated Washington's position that the Europeans had interests different from ours and that we would resist any attempt on their part to extend their system to this hemisphere. He also assured the world that we had no interest in interfering with any existing European colonies on this side of the Atlantic and promised that we would refrain from interfering in European wars that did not involve us.

The message, well received in the United States, brought various reactions from Europe. The English, in general, were pleased. The Austrians and Russians were furious, the French were divided, and the Spanish seemed unconcerned. The American ambassador to Madrid was dumfounded at the lack of interest in a document so vital to Spain. Also surprising was the lack of comment from South America. Although Latin Americans appreciated an interest in their welfare, they no more wanted interference from the United States than they wanted it from the powers of Europe.

The Era of Good Feelings

The growing spirit of nationalism in postwar America was shown at home as well as abroad. While the diplomats were busy molding an American foreign policy, their countrymen turned the land into a hive of economic activity. It was the day of the turnpike, the canal, and the earliest railroads. In the Northwest, frontiersmen hacked away at the wilderness, clearing new holdings, building settlements, and driving back the Indian population. In the South, an empire known as the Cotton Kingdom was developing fast, tremendously stimulated by Eli Whitney's 1793 invention of a machine to separate seeds from cotton.

The years following the War of 1812 were characterized as the Era of Good Feelings. The Democratic-Republicans (as the party of Jefferson, Madison, and Monroe was called until about 1828, when it became the Democratic Party) were still in power, as the Federalists had dug their political graves by fruitless opposition to the war. A predominantly Democratic-Republican Congress passed America's first protective tariff in 1816, taking its lead from Hamilton's earlier *Report on Manufacturing.* They also stole Federalist thunder by rechartering the Bank of the United States in

1816. Foreign-policy questions, once a main point of difference between the two parties, were no longer in the forefront. Napoleon was exiled to St. Helena, and Europe was busy restoring its unemployed monarchs to their former positions. In general, with Democratic-Republicans acting and talking like Federalists, there seemed to be little occasion for further factional strife on the political scene.

The indomitable John Marshall

Yet in this predominantly Jeffersonian era, it was a Federalist who led the nationalists in establishing a strong central government. John Marshall firmly believed that the United States was a federal unit, not a confederation or an association of states that grudgingly allotted power to the central government. Early in his career as Chief Justice, he gave warning that he held far-reaching judicial opinions. His verdict in the 1803 case of *Marbury vs. Madison,* asserting that the court had the power to declare the laws of Congress unconstitutional, marked out the field of battle.

The decade following the War of 1812 saw Marshall at his best. His quick sense of humor, his lack of pretension, and his democratic conduct with his associates won their respect. They chuckled over the story of a Richmond resident who approached the shabbily dressed Chief Justice and, thinking him out of work, offered him a coin to carry a bundle. Much amused, Marshall gravely took the

John Marshall was the third Chief Justice, but he established the court's prestige.

bundle and meekly padded along behind his new employer, to the delight of those who knew him.

During the postwar years, Marshall handed down decision after decision that strengthened the position of the federal judiciary. Earlier, in 1810, he had denied the state legislature of Georgia the privilege of rescinding a contract to sell some land. In 1819, the Dartmouth College case presented a similar question. The state legislature attempted to amend a charter given to the college in colonial days, in order to have some control over its operations. Marshall held that the charter was a contract, that the college was not a civil institution participating in government, and that the legislature had no right to intervene. The modern significance is that the charter of a corporation is considered to be a contract, as that word is used in the Constitution.

Marshall came to grips even more directly with the states in cases like that of *Cohens vs. Virginia* (1821). In this complicated case, Marshall sided with Virginia, but he took the opportunity to express his opinion of the nature of the Union. He made clear the supremacy of the federal judiciary over any state judiciary, even though it might agree with a state court's opinion.

Maryland also tried to defy the Chief Justice. In 1819, it passed a law providing that if a branch of the Bank of the United States were established in that state without permission, its notes would be taxed. The federal case that resulted, *McCulloch vs. Maryland,* was perhaps Marshall's greatest. The decision of the Supreme Court denied the right of a state to tax an agency of the central government, and Marshall used the case to further define the government's position: "Let the end be legitimate, let it be within the scope of the Constitution, and all means which are appropriate, which are plainly adapted to that end, which are not prohibited, but consistent with the letter and the spirit of the Constitution, are constitutional," wrote the Chief Justice in what is perhaps the best definition of implied powers we have. In stating "The power to tax involves the power to destroy," he pointed out the dangers of placing state sovereignty above that of the federal government.

In such cases, Marshall struck at powers claimed by individual states—powers that he regarded as an invasion of the government's jurisdiction. In other rulings, he stepped forward, staking out new claims for the government, establishing precedents that would enhance its prestige. The most famous of these is *Gibbons vs. Ogden,* in which the court asserted the power of the government to regulate interstate commerce. The contest centered upon Ogden, who was trying to prevent Gibbons from operating rival steamboats between New York City and the New Jersey ports. Ogden claimed he had a monopoly from the state that gave him a prior right over Gibbons, who had a federal license. Marshall's ruling, in 1824, was that Ogden was wrong—that Congress had the power to regulate commerce whenever it crossed state boundaries. He

held that such jurisdiction affected passengers as well as goods. It was a decision of far-reaching implications. It set a precedent for subsequent governmental control over railroads, airlines, telephone and telegraph companies, power lines, and radio and television transmission.

Another case affecting commerce on the national level was that of *Brown vs. Maryland,* argued in 1827. The Chief Justice ruled that as long as goods imported into any state from abroad remained in the hands of the importer in the original package, they were not subject to state tax. The so-called Original-Package Case implied that a state's attempt to tax such packages was an attempt to regulate the nation's foreign commerce, a right reserved to the central government.

Decisions of such magnitude and implication naturally provoked criticism from the guardians of states'

The area of dispute in the case of Gibbons vs. Ogden *is shown in this 1837 view of New York from Brooklyn Heights with the shores of New Jersey in the distance.*

rights. A Senator from Kentucky, for example, passionately charged that the court was a "place above the control of the will of the people, in a state of disconnection with them, inaccessible to the charities and sympathies of human life."

Despite such complaints, most of Marshall's decisions fitted the spirit of nationalism pervading America in the early 19th century. They were also in agreement with the economic expansion of the day. Growing America, whose vast stretches were being interlaced by a transportation network, did not complain when court decisions favored its development. Men were making fortunes from young and lusty industries, and it was only natural that they wanted to retain their gains. If the Supreme Court appeared to be emerging as the stronghold of conservative America, businessmen gave it their blessing.

Underlying sectionalism

In the American air of nationalism there was a throbbing beat of sectionalism that would one day rise to a crescendo and become the major theme. On the surface of everyday events, the dominant feature of national life appeared to be its magnificent expansion. New states came quickly into the Union after the War of 1812—six of them in six years. But so fast was the country developing that the result was weakness rather than strength. New England became a strong commercial empire in itself.

The Northwest, agricultural in the main, grew jealous of its own interests. And the South, where cotton was king, developed a sectional pride that transcended national feeling. As Frederick Jackson Turner, the great historian of the American frontier, put it, the country was dividing itself into vast physiographic provinces. Each felt itself in competition with another part of the nation, convinced that the central government favored one or more of its rivals.

John C. Calhoun, later to represent the most rabid of the sectionalists, showed concern at the growing divisions of interest as early as 1817. "We are greatly and rapidly—I was about to say fearfully—growing," he remarked. "This is our pride and our danger; our weakness and our strength." This was the same Calhoun who within a decade was complaining that the system of separate geographical areas was not sufficiently recognized.

The pressure of dissent was by no means centered in the South. During the years after 1815, the West was in the normal financial turmoil that any frontier area experiences. Money was scarce, land prices were a subject of complaint, and the internal-improvement program moved much too slowly for Westerners eager for land and trade. The panic of 1819 brought the condition into sharp focus, resulting in a storm of protest from the frontiersmen. They were momentarily silenced by the land law of 1820, which

Marshall and the other six members of the Supreme Court appear on the dais at the left rear of the House of Representatives, as painted by S.F.B. Morse in 1822.

cut the minimum cost to $1.25 an acre and the minimum acreage they could buy to 80. This law was meant to help the small farmer acquire land, but the provision substituting cash payment for the customary credit soured the new terms. Even if a Westerner now could buy a farm for $100, that amount of cash was hard to come by. East-West antagonisms were multiplying to such an extent that only a larger, and more dramatic, irritation could submerge the trouble.

It appeared before long. Ironically, it came from one aspect of America's exuberant nationalism—the rapid expansion. At the birth of the national government in 1789, the population balance between North and South was almost even; by 1819, the scales had shifted. There were over 5,000,000 people in the North to about 4,500,000 in the South. Although representation in the Senate stayed even, the House had 105 Northern Representatives to 81 Southerners. The question of political power, soon to be contested by these two great sections, first came to a test in neither of them. Missouri, then a frontier territory, was the crucible in which the elements of the coming battle were fused.

The people of Missouri applied for admission to the Union in 1818, and their request was referred to Congress. A New York Representative, James Tallmadge, moved that the request be granted. He introduced an amendment, however, providing that no more slaves would be introduced

375

into the new state and that all children born into slavery in Missouri after its admission to the Union should become free at the age of 25. With that, the fat was in the fire. The amendment passed the House but lost in the Senate, and in the process became an issue of national interest. Southerners at once maintained that Congress could not pose conditions for the entrance of new states, and Northerners answered by citing such examples as Ohio, Indiana, and Illinois, whose people had to observe stipulations laid down in the Northwest Ordinance. The sixth article of that document had prohibited slavery.

The question of Missouri's statehood appeared in Congress again in the fall of 1819 and continued into the winter, with Congressmen from each major section hurling oratorical thunderbolts right and left. At the height of the excitement, residents of that part of Massachusetts known as Maine asked permission to form a state. Politicians now conceived the idea of carrying Missouri into the Union on the back of Maine. Arguments over the slave issue were temporarily resolved when Senator Jesse Thomas of Illinois proposed the famous "36–30" amendment, whereby slavery would be permitted in Missouri but prohibited elsewhere north of 36° 30′ latitude. It was the heart of the final settlement. By the spring of 1820, Maine was admitted as a free state, and after more than a year of additional wrangling, Missouri came into the Union

on the terms of the Thomas amendment.

While most proslavery men then felt that Congress could prohibit slavery on land the government owned and out of which states would come, they continued to insist it could not impose conditions upon states when they sought admission to the Union. John Quincy Adams, a New Englander, thought they were right. It was he who shrewdly observed, "The discussion of the Missouri question disclosed a secret; it revealed the basis for a new organization of parties. Here was a new party ready-formed— terrible to the whole Union, but portentously terrible to the South." Although the new party—the Republican —would not be formed until 1854, the issue had now arisen, and for the next three decades the elements of a great national struggle would, one by one, fall into place.

Thus the Era of Good Feelings was in some respects a misnomer. The principal current of America's progress during the years following the War of 1812 emphasized expansion, the growth of the central government's power, and economic development. But strong undercurrents and eddies of sectional discord indicated that nationalism was merely the surface manifestation of the young and ebullient nation. Under this bright surface was a turmoil of conflicting emotions. Not many years hence they would burst forth upon a startled world as the American Civil War.

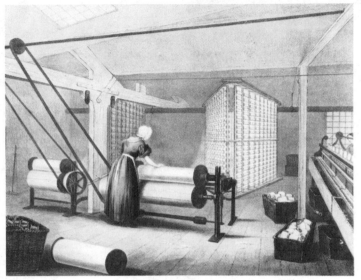

STIRRINGS
OF INDUSTRY

The Industrial Revolution that had swept England in the 18th century came late to America, a country that had been mainly concerned with agriculture. It was in the early 19th century that the United States began to settle the problems involved in simply existing as a new nation and to set about producing its own goods for consumption, such as textiles for clothing, machinery for farming, and vehicles for transportation. The beginnings of industry were difficult. Americans lacked the means to process raw materials and were slow to respond to the conceptions of men like Peter Cooper and Robert Fulton. But it was not long before the American mind ably applied itself to the challenge of industry. It was in the early activities of the men in this portfolio—men of imagination, courage, and conviction—that the seeds of industrial America were sown that have resulted in today's great mechanized society.

WHEELS TURN

Eli Whitney's revolutionary cotton gin, a device to remove seeds from cotton, is operated (above, left) on a plantation.

Mass production, the American industrial development that would one day sweep the world, was born in the Connecticut factory above. Here, in 1798, Eli Whitney used the machines he had invented, like the drill press (right), to make interchangeable parts, assembled later into rifles.

New England textile mills (left) mushroomed as bales of cotton from the gins of the South poured into Northern cities.

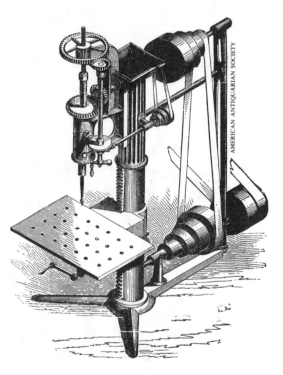

AMERICAN ANTIQUARIAN SOCIETY

379

AMERICA'S FIRST FACTORY

In 1789, Samuel Slater (above), a cotton spinner's apprentice with ambition and a good memory, slipped out of England and came to the United States with a valuable secret locked in his head. He had memorized the designs of England's most modern and carefully guarded textile machinery. (He could not risk drawing plans of it, for this was a criminal offense in England.) In the tall, narrow building (left), Moses Brown's mill in Pawtucket, Rhode Island, Slater struggled, with two machinists and a wheelwright, to make the intricate Arkwright spinning frame below. In 1790, this equipment went into operation, and the first factory in the United States was turning out spindles of cotton yarn.

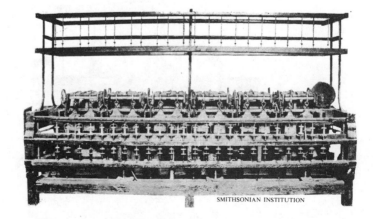

STEAM MOVES IN

TRANSPORTATION LIBRARY, UNIVERSITY OF MICHIGAN

Oliver Evans (above) and Robert Fulton (below) were both pioneers in harnessing the great energy of the new steam engine.

Evans and Fulton suffered the fate of most visionaries—the snickers and the gibes of those who couldn't imagine ships without sails and horseless carriages. Although Evans' steam-powered Orukter Amphibolos (amphibious dredge) at the left looked strange indeed in 1803, it worked—and on land and water. Fulton, a talented painter as well as a brilliant engineer, was determined to prove to an age devoted to sailing ships that steam would propel ships of the future. His steamship *Clermont* (above) lacked the grace of a clipper ship, but in 1807 it successfully puffed its way up the Hudson River from New York City to Albany.

STIRRINGS OF INDUSTRY

McCORMICK'S REAPER

The American farm moved toward mechanization in 1831, when Cyrus McCormick's reaper was first demonstrated successfully in a wheat field in Virginia. Incredulous onlookers saw the horsepowered implement cut six times as much grain in a day as a single farm hand could cut with a scythe.

Peter Cooper was one of America's first great
industrialists and a New York civic leader.

THE TRAIN
TAKES OVER

In 1830, Cooper's one-horsepower railroad steam engine, the *Tom Thumb,* pulled a car of spectators (below) in a race with a horse-drawn car. Although the horse won this race because of a mechanical failure in the engine, the inventor had convinced many people that railways were the transportation of the future. Within a few decades, cars hauled by puffing locomotives (above) would supersede covered wagons in America's Far West.

The steel for America's first locomotives was forged at the West Point

Foundry, which began to work iron in 1818 in Cold Spring, New York.

CHAPTER 14

THE JACKSONIANS

The currents of conflict beneath the surface of the Era of Good Feelings began to break into the open as the election of 1824 drew near.

Before that election, New Englanders had watched the South maintain political dominance with an unbroken string of Virginians as successful Presidential candidates. Now their hope lay in a member of the old Adams family, John Quincy, whose reputation might bring the Presidency to a New Englander. He did not appeal to the frontier as a backwoodsman would have, but neither did he represent the Federalists of the commercial class. He was broadly educated, with wide experience in the diplomatic field, and his character was impeccable. Historian Frederick Jackson Turner says that Adams had Puritan restraint, self-scrutiny, and self-condemnation. Adams' own self-assessment was "I am a man of reserved, cold, austere, and forbidding manners."

Adams' quest for the Presidency was not an easy one. A number of

Andrew Jackson, painted here by Alonzo Chappel, became a national hero after defeating the British at New Orleans in 1815.

widely popular political figures on the scene offered him sharp competition. Henry Clay, Speaker of the House—known as Harry of the West—had a large following, as did a fellow Westerner, Andrew Jackson. Southerners like William Crawford of Georgia and John C. Calhoun of South Carolina were also contenders.

Adams regarded Clay and Jackson with distaste. Clay, a Kentuckian, represented a way of life that a proper New Englander like Adams found objectionable. Clay was fond of horse racing, had no objection to the social glass, and played both poker and politics with enthusiasm and skill. His manner pleased many voters, and his ability as a compromiser and his interest in internal improvements pleased others. Andrew Jackson was even more Western than Clay. Those who worshiped the hero of New Orleans crossed all party lines and geographical boundaries.

Such competition did not deter Adams, who quietly built support as his followers reminded voters of his achievements as Secretary of State under Monroe. The acquisition of Florida in 1819, and Spain's relin-

John Quincy Adams, though capable, was a frustrated President.

quishment of its claims north of the 42nd parallel, attributed to Adams' diplomacy, gained him favor.

The Missouri Compromise, which Adams referred to as a "flaming sword," politically affected all the aspirants. Crawford lost strength by his states'-rights stand; Clay's compromises cost him votes in both the North and the South; Calhoun, a Southerner, likewise suffered. Jackson was the least affected. During the height of the Missouri controversy he was busy in Florida fighting Indians and hanging Englishmen, an undertaking that had strong appeal to the nationalist voter.

Adams, however, actually benefited from the Missouri Compromise; it helped to install him as the Northern candidate. Privately he condemned slavery; publicly he had, for constitutional reasons, opposed any restrictions upon Missouri's entrance into the Union—a stand that had Southerners applauding.

When the 1824 election results were in, Jackson had 99 electoral votes, and Adams had 84. Because neither had a majority, the contest was thrown into the House of Representatives as is provided for in the Twelfth Amendment. Clay, who had run last, now threw his support to Adams, who was elected.

When Clay was appointed Secretary of State, the cry of corruption was raised. John Randolph of Virginia complained publicly to such an extent that he found himself in a duel with Clay. As they were both poor shots, the affray ended with no casualties. Jackson, although himself somewhat given to duels, kept his pistols encased and grimly planned his next battle—the election of 1828.

The administration of John Quincy Adams was generally unsatisfactory, and no one was more disappointed in it than the President himself. Although his previous success had been in diplomacy, he now found his foreign-affairs program the most seriously blocked. The United States Congress, filled with Adams' enemies, including many Jackson supporters, did little to help him. When the President wanted to send representatives to an international meeting held at Panama, Congress debated so long over their appointment that America was not represented. Great Britain, meanwhile, was represented thoroughly and lost no time in furthering commercial relationships with South America.

Adams tried to contain his dissatisfaction, but having cast aside the practice of distributing government jobs in return for support, he had no weapon with which to maintain control. Other men might use personal magnetism, but Adams had none. Lonely and introspective, he confided more and more in his beloved diary.

The return of Andy Jackson

After Jackson's defeat in the Presidential contest of 1824–25, he resigned his seat in Congress and spent the next three years readying himself for the battle of 1828. His efforts, aided by Adams' failure, were successful. His victory in the election was overwhelming, and early in 1829 he made his return to Washington.

On Inauguration Day the capital was jammed with milling crowds. Daniel Webster made the gloomy remark that "They seem to think the country is rescued from some dreadful danger." He and others recoiled as roughhewn Jackson admirers jostled one another in the White House, upsetting pails of orange punch, breaking glasses, and climbing on the furniture with their muddy boots for a better look at Old Hickory.

The people's hero was now in power, and the people demanded a share of the victory. The lower classes

Jackson's many executions of army deserters and his destruction of personal enemies were attacked in this 1828 cartoon.

felt that rotation in office was not only part of the political game but that it was in keeping with the democratic principle of government.

Jackson agreed. Historically, he has been charged with starting the spoils system. He did not invent it, nor did he make excessive use of it. From George Washington's time it was customary to appoint to office one's supporters. Jackson's successors to the Presidency were to make him look as if he showed no favoritism at all when it came to handing out political jobs.

Old Hickory was typically Western in his informality. As soon as he was in office, the nation witnessed a sample of this method. Turning to his closest friends, the President gathered around him an unofficial group referred to derisively by his enemies as the "kitchen cabinet," and here national policy was made. The kitchen cabinet, chosen by Jackson wholly without partisan considerations, functioned smoothly enough, but the official cabinet soon became a problem that threatened the very existence of the new regime. A woman was at the bottom of the trouble. Her name was Peggy O'Neale Timberlake Eaton, and her place in American politics is unique.

The controversy started on January 1, 1829, when Jackson's Tennessee friend and future secretary of War, John H. Eaton, married Peggy, once a barmaid. An attractive young widow of a navy purser who had never returned from sea, she was an old friend of Andy Jackson's. Eaton had known Peggy well when she was still married to her first husband. Some accounts say that he married her on Jackson's advice in order to quiet gossipers.

It was Mrs. John C. Calhoun, wife of the Vice-President, who led the assault. She refused to call on Eaton's bride and made it clear that she considered the former Mrs. Timberlake unqualified to hold the social position into which she had married. The other cabinet wives, as well as a number of Washington ladies who were engaged in the struggle for prestige, joined up for the duration.

The free-for-all that ensued might have done little harm had not male reserves been called up. In the midst of the fray was Vice-President John Calhoun, who, wanting to be Presi-

dent, believed he had only to wait for his chance to succeed to that office. But he became impatient and tried to increase the odds in his favor. There were two or three members of Jackson's cabinet whom he regarded as enemies. One was Secretary of State Martin Van Buren, who was also a Presidential possibility. Behind him stood John Eaton and William Barry, the Postmaster General. By helping to create an incident out of Eaton's choice of a wife, Calhoun hoped to break up the cabinet, embarrass the administration, and so improve his chances for the Presidency.

The plan worked well enough at first. The gallant Van Buren rushed to Peggy's defense, his own arm extended in proffered support at all social functions. Some say this simple gesture made him President of the United States, for Jackson was enormously pleased by such open loyalty.

If Calhoun was out to wreck the cabinet for his own purposes, Van Buren was out to perform an act of political judo, using the momentum of his opponent's assault to gain victory for himself. Accordingly, one day in the spring of 1831 he suggested his own resignation. He presumed this would cause Eaton to follow, as evidence of his loyalty to Jackson, whereupon the other cabinet members, no matter how reluctant they

Symbols of Henry Clay's statecraft (right) and his life as a farmer are included in this life-size portrait by John Neagle.

THE CAPITOL

Jackson's Indian policy forced most Eastern tribes across the Mississippi over what became known as the Trail of Tears.

were, would feel they must resign also.

The scheme worked to perfection, and before long Jackson had the opportunity to reconstruct his cabinet, free from any Calhoun influence. Van Buren was rewarded with an appointment as minister to England, but the Senate, with Vice-President Calhoun casting the deciding vote, blocked his confirmation. This only heightened his popularity and standing in the Democratic Party, and the result was his immediate nomination and election to the Vice-Presidency on the Jackson ticket in 1832. He was now the heir apparent to Jackson's political crown. All he had to do was wait quietly until 1836. In 1832, Calhoun had resigned the Vice-Presidency to go back home and, as Senator, carry on the fight.

Old Hickory loses some supporters

Before Jackson had been long in office, some Westerners began to wonder if the hero of New Orleans was as much their man as they had once thought. As Senator he had voted for federal support of such improvements as roads and canals in the American interior. As President he veered toward the strict constructionist point of view that some projects merited government assistance but that many more were too local to justify it. In improvements to river navigation, for example, he held that only projects benefiting two or more states could be considered of national importance and would get his support.

Before long there came before him a bill proposing a federal grant of $150,000 to aid in the construction of a road between Maysville, Kentucky, and the Ohio River, right through the heart of Jackson country and connecting Kentucky with the East. To the dismay of Westerners, the President vetoed the bill. In his veto message Jackson argued that the proposed road was to run altogether within the limits of a state, "conferring partial instead of general advantages."

The storm of protest was answered by the President's defenders, who pointed out that on the day of the veto—May 31, 1830—he approved a $130,000 expenditure to survey and extend the Cumberland Road running west from Maryland through Pennsylvania, Ohio, Indiana, and Illinois.

Jackson insisted that he was not hostile to internal improvements, if they were of national scope.

As for land and monetary policies, subjects on which Westerners were particularly touchy, Jackson also perplexed his fellows. Although he was an advocate of paper money, so popular among the inflation-minded frontiersmen, the President began to grow concerned about its extensive circulation. By the early 1830s, Western banks were printing unbacked paper money at a rate that threatened economic stability, and so rampant was the speculation that Jackson stepped in with federal control. In an order of July 11, 1836, called the Specie Circular, he dealt Westerners a severe blow by decreeing that public lands could be bought only with hard money, or specie. Western banks were the hardest hit, and in the financial contraction that followed, many were forced to close. Land sales fell off. When the panic came in 1837, frontiersmen were quick to blame the Specie Circular. So loud were the complaints that the order was withdrawn in 1838.

In other respects, Jackson's land policy pleased his farmer neighbors. During the years he was in office, almost 64,000,000 acres of public domain were disposed of by means of individual sales and grants to the states. In 1832, the President declared that public lands ought not to be used as a source of revenue, but should be sold at a price that barely covered administrative costs. The American government was now headed toward a policy of free land—a policy that would be realized in the Homestead Act of 1862.

In Indian affairs, Jackson held closer to the viewpoint that Americans expected of him. At the time of his administration, the Cherokees were the only powerful Indians remaining in well-settled parts of the country. Their lands in Georgia posed a problem, for although the federal government had long since recognized Cherokee property rights, the state government had annexed the tribal lands in 1828.

Jackson recommended to the Indians that they move peaceably across the Mississippi, where they would be granted new lands. The Cherokees said no. They ignored the tomahawk and, in a most savage manner, went straight to the Supreme Court of the United States. Startled, it backed away, asserting that the Indians could not sue there. A missionary named Samuel A. Worcester then arranged to bring the matter before the court in his name. In *Worcester vs. Georgia* (1832), John Marshall held that the federal government alone had jurisdiction in the domain of the Cherokee nation, and therefore the Georgia law was unconstitutional.

Georgia ignored the ruling, and when all concerned turned to Jackson for an answer, he roared, "John Marshall has made his decision, now let him enforce it." The Indians saw they were beaten and agreed to move westward, where more land and a settlement of $5,000,000 awaited them. Other tribes made similar agreements, and during Jackson's administration they journeyed over what they called the Trail of Tears to a new home.

Jackson and the Southerners

Back in the early 1820s, the South was, in general, safely national in viewpoint. Yet only 10 years were to elapse before those insisting upon states' rights would become dominant and even gain complete control of one state, South Carolina. This represented the beginning of the most serious internal conflict the United States had faced until then—a conflict that was not to be settled until the nation fought the Civil War.

The friction between the federal government and the states'-righters in South Carolina began over the tariff of 1828, which they wanted to nullify. The notion that a state could nullify a national law that it regarded as unconstitutional was not new. The Kentucky and Virginia Resolutions of 1798 had stressed the "compact" theory of government, contending that Congress had transcended its powers by passing the Alien and Sedition Acts. In 1828, Calhoun expounded a strong states'-rights position in a pamphlet called *The South Carolina Exposition and Protest*. More excitement might have resulted if the author's identity had been revealed, but it was not. The main theme of this

document was that a state might annul a law of Congress that it regarded as unconstitutional. It went further, however, and implied that the Union could be dissolved should other states follow this course.

As Southern belligerence grew, the situation came more into the national limelight. Early in 1830, Senators Robert Hayne and Daniel Webster engaged in a historic debate over the question of nullification. Americans watched with increasing interest as Jackson more fully revealed his own feelings at an important banquet in April, 1830. "Our Union, it must be preserved!" he said, when called upon for a toast. Calhoun, who had never learned the value of brevity, responded with "The Union, next to our liberty most dear! May we always remember that it can only be preserved by respecting the rights of the states and distributing equally the benefits and burdens of the Union!" The exchange did not generate much resentment in South Carolina, but the nullifiers now knew that Jackson was not in their camp.

The event that triggered an expected explosion occurred during the summer of 1831. Two Charleston merchants decided to test the constitutionality of federal tariff laws by refusing to pay certain duties. The local United States district attorney, a sympathizer, refused to prosecute them and promptly lost his job. Jackson said flatly that a state could not nullify a federal law, and he refused to appoint to the vacant position a successor who did not agree with him. Calhoun now came forward openly as South Carolina's defender, issuing a restatement of his *Exposition* and taking his stand against the administration. A head-on collision between Jackson and the Calhoun men was now inevitable.

During 1832, Jackson tried adjusting differences by supporting a revised tariff bill, but the result was a tariff regarded by Southerners as far too protective. South Carolinians especially were not to be silenced, and in November, 1832, at a convention called by the state legislature, an Ordinance of Nullification was passed. It declared that the tariff laws of 1828 and 1832 were unconstitutional, and therefore null and void. February 1, 1833, was fixed as the date when the ordinance was to become effective. The framers of the document made it clear that any attempted coercion on the part of the federal government would result in South Carolina's departure from the Union. They also forbade appeal to the Supreme Court

NEW YORK PUBLIC LIBRARY

A Northern view of South Carolina's ordinance to nullify tariffs forecasts treason, civil war, deception, and finally John Calhoun as a despot.

399

Nicholas Biddle, president of the Bank of the United States, was a victim of Jackson's enmity.

of any case involving the legality of the nullification.

Jackson was not without an answer. Even as the nullifiers were preparing to meet, the President had spoken his mind to a South Carolina legislator who was about to leave for home. "Tell them," he said, "that they can talk and write resolutions and print threats to their hearts' content. But if one drop of blood be shed there in defiance of the laws of the United States, I will hang the first man of them I can get my hands on, to the first tree I can find." One of South Carolina's Senators told Senator Thomas Hart Benton of Missouri that he doubted if Jackson would go that far. Benton, who had once dueled with the rugged Tennes-

seean, replied, "When Jackson begins to talk about hanging, they can begin to look for the ropes."

There were no hangings. Although Jackson had no compunctions about hanging a man if he thought it necessary, he did not want to antagonize South Carolina so much that other Southern states would join in open opposition to the federal government. Early in 1833, Congress passed Henry Clay's compromise tariff, sharply scaling down the duties. As a face-saver, Congress also passed the Force Bill, which authorized the President to use the armed forces to collect duties if judicial processes were obstructed. The South Carolina convention was now reassembled, and it repealed the Ordinance of Nullification. Then, to save its own face, it declared the Force Bill null and void. Thus both sides left the field of battle chanting victory. The Carolinians actually came off better, for they proved that a state could defy the federal government and obtain a change in national policy. Jackson was gloomy about the whole affair, feeling that secession would be tried again, perhaps over some other issue. "The next pretext will be the Negro or slavery question," he predicted.

The bank war

During 1832, as the nullification question mounted to a climax, a second front was opened in the political war against Jackson. It was election year, one in which his followers or-

The prosperous Second Bank of the United States, in Philadelphia, was the cause of the conflict between Biddle and Jackson, who wanted no national bank.

ganized themselves as the Democratic Party, held a national convention, and nominated their man by the delegates' vote. Anti-Jackson men took the name National Republican Party (soon to be changed to Whig) and chose Henry Clay as their candidate.

Into the Presidential campaign was thrown an issue that Jackson's opponents thought would end his political reign. Henry Clay now persuaded Nicholas Biddle, president of the Second Bank of the United States, to apply for a recharter of that institution in the hope that Jackson's known opposition to the bank would help to defeat him at the polls.

The Second B.U.S., as it was called, had been chartered for a period of 20 years in 1816. After 1823, Biddle, a Philadelphian and a man of letters, was its president. He was opposed by the Jackson men, who were not above attacking his institution on the ground that it was a financial octopus used against the President politically. Jackson himself, in his first annual message to Congress, questioned both the constitutionality of the bank and its ability to establish a uniform and sound currency. The Supreme Court already had ruled upon the first point; on the second, Jackson was decidedly unfair. But this did not detract from the public popularity of his stand.

Despite the nullification question and Henry Clay's carefully contrived bank issue, Jackson won a second

Jackson attacks the many-headed bank hydra with his veto stick. The largest head is Biddle; the others represent the directors of the state branches.

great victory at the polls in 1832. With it, he carried Van Buren into the Vice-Presidency and further strengthened the New Yorker's claim as Jackson's successor. Among the losers was Nicholas Biddle. Tough-minded Old Hickory now demonstrated his lack of sympathy for known enemies by removing federal deposits of between $10,000,000 and $12,000,000 from the Second B.U.S. several years before its charter expired. He scattered this financial largesse around among some selected state banks that promptly were referred to as "pet banks." Although the action caused a serious dislocation in financial circles, and destroyed an organization that was not to be replaced until the establishment of the Federal Reserve System 75 years later, Jackson had his way.

Jacksonian diplomacy

In the field of foreign affairs, Jackson was as direct and forthright as ever. In his first inaugural address, the hero of New Orleans and subjugator of the British was as mild as a lamb, promising to preserve international peace and to cultivate friendship to the best of his ability. The world could not argue with his purpose "to ask nothing that is not clearly right and to submit to nothing that is wrong." Jackson, however, was a man rather easily offended, and his interpretation of when he was wronged did not always coincide with that of the other party.

One of the first diplomatic questions to come up in his administration concerned Great Britain. From the days of the Revolution, the Americans had looked longingly at the West Indian trade, from which they were excluded since leaving the Empire. In

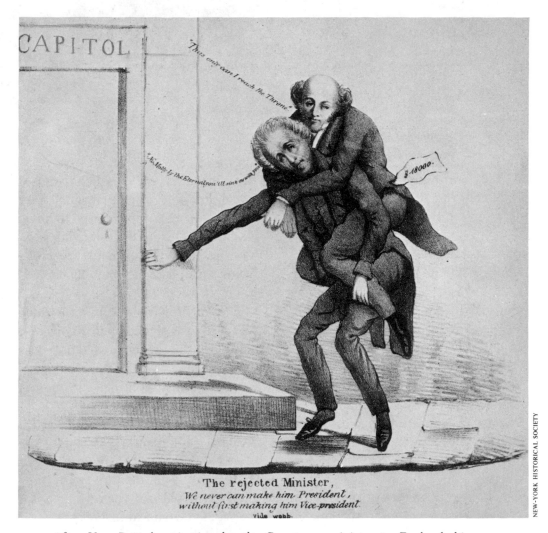

The rejected Minister,
We never can make him President,
without first making him Vice-president.
vide webb.

After Van Buren's rejection by the Senate as minister to England, his enemies sharply mocked Jackson's effort to carry him along to the White House.

Jackson's strong-arm demand for payment from France's King Louis Philippe for losses suffered during the Napoleonic Wars is lampooned in this print.

1822, Britain had opened the door a crack, charging American goods heavy duties and still forbidding some articles. After bickering between the two countries, during the Adams administration, Britain again stopped the trade. Jackson now took hold of the knotty problem, politely asking on the one hand for a renewal and on the other threatening nonintercourse between the United States and Canada. The bluff worked. By 1830, he had what he wanted; ships again plied the waters between the British West Indies and the American coast.

With France, he was more violent. American businessmen had claims against the French government dating back to the spoliations of commerce in the Napoleonic days, but had not been able to get a settlement. The

Revolution of 1830, which brought Louis Philippe to the throne, gave Jackson a fresh opportunity to press his claims. During the following summer, a treaty was made whereby France promised to pay 25,000,000 francs in six installments.

The spirit of friendship with which the treaty was signed cooled considerably when the French missed their first payment. For a year or so, the American government continued to request payment from the French. Then Jackson recommended reprisals on French property, commenting, "I know the French—they won't pay unless they're made to." The debtors were now highly incensed and vowed that not a sou would be paid until Jackson apologized. He was reported to have roared, "Apologize! I'd see the whole

404

race roasting in hell first!" The French minister, Alphonse Pageot, took his wife, who was the daughter of Major William B. Lewis of the kitchen cabinet, and his son, Andrew Jackson Pageot, back to France. The diplomatic impasse seemed complete.

While Jackson fumed and the French pouted, Great Britain stepped in with an offer to arbitrate. In February, 1836, after Jackson had made a left-handed apology, and the reluctant French were brought around, the offer was accepted. The position of the British arose more out of expediency than generosity, for they did not want to see their ally, France, involved in a needless war with the United States. By early May, Jackson blandly told his countrymen that the diplomatic victory was his: The arrearage had been paid up—and paid with interest.

To a good many Americans of his day, Andrew Jackson was an enigma. On the surface he appeared to be a typically direct and open-mannered Westerner, understanding and easily understood. But beneath this apparent simplicity swirled emotional eddies and crosscurrents that made him sometimes unpredictable. He had studied law, but he had not developed a judicial mind. His actions were more likely to be emotional and unrestrained than thoughtful and controlled. His facility with the English language was remarkable, considering the limitations of his background, and he was to produce some of the ablest state papers of his time. He has no counterpart in European history, and it would be hard to find his parallel

The Peggy O'Neale Eaton affair is gibed at in this 1834 drawing, with the former barmaid shown dancing before Jackson and his mostly unreceptive cabinet.

in the history of the United States.

One of Jackson's most impressive qualities was a recognition of his own limitations. Knowing that he was pugnacious and quick-tempered, he deliberately chose for his kitchen cabinet men who counterbalanced some of his weaknesses. This was not always enough, as is revealed by some of his feuds. His conduct in the Eaton-Calhoun battle revealed him as narrow and vindictive—traits that grew more pronounced the longer he stayed in office. After the election triumph of 1832, his demands for adulation and agreement became even greater.

As President he knew exactly what he wanted, as a single sentence from his writings indicates: "The Federal Constitution must be obeyed, states' rights preserved, our national debt must be paid, direct taxes and loans avoided, and the Federal Union preserved." His simple, direct manner appealed greatly to a politically unsophisticated people. They were to discover, as he did, that the realization of these plain-spoken aims was often a good deal more difficult than their mere enunciation.

Jackson's greatest success came not so much from the formulation of any political theory as from his remarkable ability to judge the desires of the people and to translate them into a policy easily understood by the average man. Instinctively, he seemed to plumb people's minds and to know what they wanted. When he came forth with policies shaped to these desires,

he was, of course, enormously popular. Thus, instead of commanding his followers, he simply led them in the direction they wanted to go.

The changes wrought by the Jacksonians were far broader, however, than the simple intentions expressed by the President himself. These men took a somewhat more practical view of democracy than their predecessors, the Jeffersonians, emphasizing economic equality to a generation that, having achieved something of political equality, was now concerning itself with the inequities associated with rising industrialism. Men of Jackson's day had fewer objections to government interference that would insure the workers a fair share of their toil. The common man now demanded an economic as well as a political democracy. The Jacksonians approved the workingmen's struggle for a shorter workday, favored greater guarantees of political rights for the workers, and advocated a more liberal land policy.

Historians have rather heatedly debated whether Jackson was representative of the frontier or of the rising working class in the Northeast. Each side has a good set of arguments, but the likelihood is that Jackson represented Americans as a whole, for the nation was still, to a large extent, a kind of frontier, with all the characteristics of equalitarianism attributed to a frontier society. Old Hickory, in sensing the temper of the times and living up to it, made his era known to later generations as the Age of Jackson.

NEW ROADS— THE WATERWAYS

The Louisiana Purchase of 1803 opened the land beyond the Mississippi to the frontier-loving American. The trail breakers had hewed their way into the wilderness on foot and horseback. The homesteaders who followed in their tracks were heading West to stay—they brought families, livestock, tools, seeds for the first sowing. In the early 19th century, before the railroad, the pioneer could go West two ways—by wagon and by boat. The roads of those days were few and bad. Before the coming of the steamboat, travelers were carried slowly along rivers by bargelike flatboats and keelboats. Sometimes a family that reached its new homesite aboard a flatboat used the lumber from it to build its first frontier cabin. In the 1820s, the great steamboat days on the Ohio, Mississippi, and Missouri Rivers began, overcoming the transportation obstacle and hastening the settling of the West.

This type of slow, heavy flatboat carried many homesteading families West. These boats were poled along or allowed to drift with the current of the river.

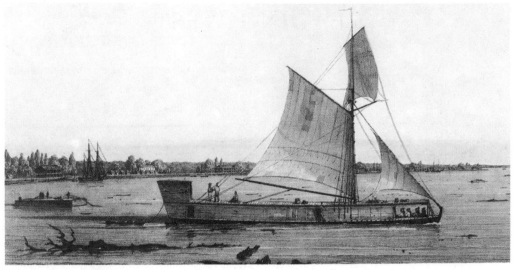

NEW ROADS—THE WATERWAYS

EARLY RIVER BOATS

Keelboats like the one above were more maneuverable and faster than flatboats and could be sailed on some rivers. The fur traders of the Missouri River country often traveled on the keelboats. They loaded them with supplies for the trip upriver, and if trapping was good, they returned downriver with a load of pelts.

The Mississippi River plantation of 1800, at the left, depended on keelboats and flatboats to send cotton to market and to bring in supplies. The keelboat in mid-river has a cargo of cotton bales. A flatboat (far left) is unloading supplies. The keelboat with the striped canopy in the foreground is a pleasure craft.

HEADING WEST

MUSEUM OF NATURAL HISTORY, LE HAVRE

The keelboat *Philanthropist* (sketched in 1825 by Charles Lesueur, who also drew the scenes opposite) heads down the Ohio. George Caleb Bingham painted Mississippi rivermen (below) playing cards as they drift along.

CITY ART MUSEUM OF ST. LOUIS

Cooking on flatboats had to be done over an open fire—one of the hazards of early river-boat travel. The "dining room," lined with bunks, on a passenger-carrying keelboat (below) was uncomfortably primitive.

NEW ROADS—THE WATERWAYS

THE COMING OF STEAM

When this water color was painted by Felix Achille Saint-Aulaire in 1821, on the banks of the Ohio, the steamboat (right) was just beginning to appear on America's great Western rivers. The slow-moving flatboats (left) and keelboats (center), long the only water transportation to the West, ultimately would give way to the faster craft.

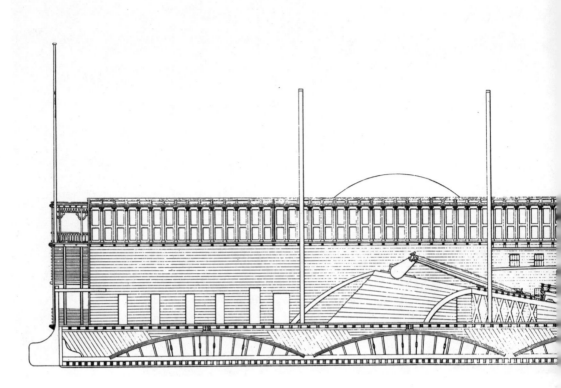

QUEENS OF THE RIVER

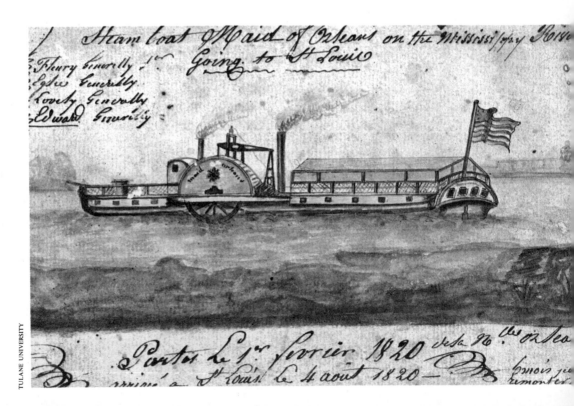

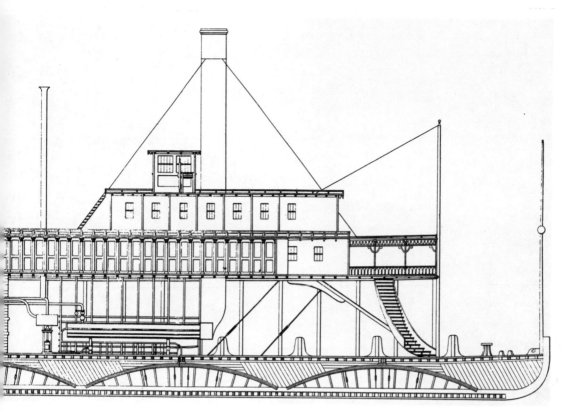

BOTH: *Transactions of the Institution of Naval Architects, 1861*

As more steamboats were built to meet the growing demand, a basic style that was used throughout the steamboat era was developed. The designer's drawing above shows a typical sidewheeler of 1861, which carried both cargo and passengers.

The drawing (right) is a cross-section of the bow of a typical Mississippi steamboat of the 1860s. Because its superstructure was always much wider than its shallow hull, the complicated system of struts and braces shown here was necessary.

This 1820 water color (opposite) of the *Maid of Orleans* is the earliest known picture of a Mississippi steamboat. Although the *Maid* was smaller and less elaborate than the boat diagramed above, she was built from a similar design.

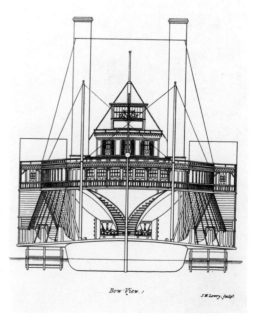

Bow View.   J.W.Lowry, sculpt.

STEAMBOATS EVERYWHERE

Pittsburgh in 1840 (above), rightly called the Gateway to the West, was a great inland port. A steady flow of homesteaders boarded the steamboats that lined the city's bustling docks. They began their journey by traveling down the Ohio River.

The steamboat, in the scene at the right, is carrying settlers and trappers on the treacherous, snag-ridden upper Missouri River, into the wilderness. A Swiss artist, Carl Bodmer, did the painting in 1833, while making the river journey.

In 1838, when this scene of life on the Mississippi (left) was painted, flatboats were coexisting, because they were cheap, with the ever-expanding fleet of steamboats on the river. Here the flatboatmen are passing the port of Cairo, Illinois.

417

STEAM BOAT *Metamora* - NEW YORK AND ALBANY STEAM BOAT PASSENGER LINE.

NEW ROADS—THE WATERWAYS

ALBANY TO NEW YORK

The great days of steamboating were not confined to the Western rivers. The Hudson River steamer *Metamora*, launched in 1846, sailed on the popular Albany-New York run.

THE CANALS

The canal boat as well as the steamboat played an important role in America's westward expansion. The Erie Canal, shown under construction at the left, was to link the Hudson River with Lake Erie.

The Erie Canal was completed in 1825. In the early days of its operation, its boats and barges were pulled by mules walking the towpath, as shown below. The locks are seen in the background.

PENNSYLVANIA RAILROAD

The route of the Pennsylvania Canal went through the Alleghenies. Boats were hoisted up inclines on railway cars (above).

Homesteaders headed for a new life in the West crowd aboard an Erie Canal barge (below) bound for Buffalo and Lake Erie.

KENNEDY GALLERIES

CHAPTER 15

SINEWS OF A NATION

During the first half of the 19th century there were industrial and commercial stirrings on the American scene that anticipated fundamental changes in national development. From our earliest beginnings we were primarily an agricultural people, but during these years of the middle period manufacturing and transportation took firm root, foreshadowing a day when the honest plowman would no longer be the dominant economic figure. The transition was slow, almost imperceptible at times, but it was steady. After the Civil War the change would be much faster and more apparent.

There were those who early recognized the need for strong industrial sinews, and they tried to nurse along our weak beginnings. Alexander Hamilton, in his *Report on Manufactures* in 1791, attempted to educate his countrymen on the subject. He pointed out that while we were predominantly agricultural and rural, there were advantages to be had from a more indus-

St. Louis looked like this in the 1850s. The Dred Scott case first came to trial in the white-domed building. at the right.

trialized economy. An increase in local manufacturing would stimulate immigration, provide a larger domestic market for home-grown foodstuffs, and generally strengthen the nation. These desirable goals had long been blocked by difficult obstacles. Skilled labor was scarce; unskilled labor tended to migrate westward onto cheap lands; inadequate transportation facilities could not distribute properly any kind of manufactures. To compound difficulties, the agricultural class was suspicious of the business world and reluctant to vote capital to help those who were regarded as enemies.

Time would alter the situation. In 1790 the population was about 4,000,000, most of it huddled along the seaboard. By 1850 it was approximately 24,000,000, and a great many of these people lived west of the Appalachians, where the demand for transportation to the East was great. Westerners, and even Easterners, now were quicker to accept American-made products than they had been in an earlier day. Before the War of 1812 we were still mostly dependent upon British manufactures. But the

Napoleonic Wars, and the embargo of Jefferson's time, drove a good many New Englanders into manufacturing. After the War of 1812 they demanded, and received, tariff protection. From that point on, locally manufactured items gradually took the place of imported products, and the ultimate success of American production was assured.

Advances in manufacturing were slow at first. Production was carried

Through the time of Jefferson, the only important source of industrial power other than the water wheel was a windmill like this American one of 1830.

424

In the 1800s, most American roads were primitive trails through valleys and around nature's obstacles, like this one painted by Benjamin Latrobe.

on by the "putting-out" system, in which rural folks made shoes, spun yarn, or made cloth out of materials distributed by local entrepreneurs. Gradually these workers were gathered together under a single roof to improve the quality of workmanship and to eliminate some of the unevenness of the product. By the '40s, for example, many shoe manufacturers began to offer a refinement: They produced right and left shoes, with some reference to foot sizes. The new "crooked shoe" was regarded as quite an improvement over the old "straights."

In other industries, such as that of flour milling, there were advances. As early as the 18th century certain labor-saving milling methods were patented, and with the growing demand for wheat products, millers could offer their customers better service and an improved product. Yet distribution was confined to relatively small sales areas, awaiting a break in the transportation bottleneck.

Prior to the 1850s, America's industrial world bore little resemblance to that which we know today. It was made up of small plants and home manufactures, and supported by a local market. A few places assumed a position of supremacy because of favorable geography. New England textile mills, for example, took advantage of water-power sites and the growing mill towns clustered around them. In the West, Cincinnati's position on the Ohio River (it was also served by canals and rails) gave it such a lead as a meat-packing center that it came to be called Porkopolis. Another "Western" town, Rochester, New York, grew into an important milling center because of its water power and its accessibility to both the Great Lakes and New York City by way of the Erie Canal. Geography also dictated the rise of St. Louis as a commercial capital. Located near the confluence of the Missouri and Mississippi Rivers, it became important at an early date.

Hamilton's prediction that the erection of factories would increase immigration was only partly fulfilled. Cheap land probably accounted for the movement of most people from Europe to America. There were, however, a good many who lingered in the city, unable or unwilling to go on in search of a farmstead. Shortly after the War of 1812 a steady flow of immigrants began to enter the port of New York, a movement that accelerated during the century. Shipping lines did a big business hauling in prospective Americans, not all of whom became farmers. Those with technical skills were encouraged to take jobs in the rising factory system, and they did much to improve the productivity of young industries. Rather than industry encouraging immigration, it was immigration that encouraged industry for a while, because large-scale manufacturing could

not have developed without a solid labor base, concentrated at sources of power and transportation. Much later, toward the end of the 19th century, Hamilton's thesis that manufacturing would encourage immigration would be more valid.

Roots of a factory system

Overshadowed by such national movements as westward expansion or the rise of sectionalism, the growth of American industrial cities was relatively unnoticed during the first half of the 19th century. Yet during these years changes took place very rapidly indeed. One explanation is the alacrity with which Americans accepted mechanization. In England it met opposition because it meant technological unemployment. Here, where there was a labor shortage, machines were welcomed. By 1840 there were some 1,200 cotton factories in this country, most of them in the Northeast. Around them had sprouted factory towns that offered inducements to prospective mill hands.

Not all of our industries grew as rapidly as cotton-textile manufacturing. Our attempts to compete with the English woolen mills had little success before 1860, despite the efforts of Congressmen to provide tariff protection. It was impossible to legislate tastes, and Americans continued to show a preference for English wool.

Nor did the iron industry develop overnight into a full-grown branch of the economy. Textile machinery could be run by water power, but iron foundries needed coal and coke. Our search for a suitable coking coal was a long one, and progress was slow. Pig-iron production grew tenfold during the middle period, but even so, we could boast of only about a half-million tons a year when England was producing 3,000,000 tons annually. The American effort was largely confined to making iron pipes, cast-iron stoves, nails, and other small manufactures. The age of steel would not emerge until after the Civil War. Until then our demands far outran our capacity to refine metals.

During these infant years the fledgling industries tried to develop a sufficient labor force. The problem was greater than one might suppose. Not only were cheap lands drawing off potential mill hands in a land that was characteristically agricultural, but the unsavory reputation of working conditions in the English mills frightened away many who considered employment in our new industries. Mill owners did all they could to make factory work more attractive. New England farm girls were given to understand that life in a textile factory was akin to that of a finishing school. Instruction in the social graces and foreign languages was offered after hours. Parents were promised that the girls would be strictly supervised, both at work and at boarding houses managed by respectable ladies, pref-

In 1853, Cincinnati, Ohio, was called the Queen City of the West, for then it was still considered Western and was the largest community in its area.

erably widows with small children. Thousands of young women were induced to accept such employment. It offered them an opportunity to learn a trade and be self-supporting.

The use of women and children in industry, the growth of immigration after 1820, and popular hostility to unions expressed in anticonspiracy laws made it hopeless for labor to try to organize. Employers quickly assumed complete control and called the play at every turn. As early as 1825 nearly all adult males were entitled to vote, and there was thus a possibility of achieving gains at the ballot box. But even here the results were disappointing. The most the workers could hope for was the ideal of the 10-hour day, and even that would not be achieved without a struggle. Collective bargaining through some sort of labor union was just a hazy, dimly visualized theory.

Horsepower on the highways

Throughout colonial and postcolonial days America's inland transportation was indeed primitive. The original 13 colonies fixed their eyes upon the sea, and thought in terms of international trade. Those who chose to engage in trade between colonies, and later between states, believed that the Atlantic Ocean was the best and cheapest thoroughfare. There was no adequate network of roads linking together the political units that became the United States. Nor did there seem to be much pros-

By 1850, heavy industry had already begun to specialize, as shown by the Novelty Iron Works in New York, makers of boilers and engines for steamers.

Women going to work in an early New England mill in a rustic setting, as painted by Winslow Homer, shows the change from agriculture to manufacturing.

pect that this deficiency would be soon remedied.

A few rivers, such as the Hudson and the Delaware, were navigable for varying distances, but in the South and in New England the fall line was too close to the sea to make river transport feasible. West of the great Appalachian Range there were possibilities in such broad and important rivers as the Ohio, or along the Great Lakes that stretched out for hundreds of miles. But between the Atlantic seaboard and these waterways lay forbidding mountains. Somehow, they would have to be breached.

For a long time most Americans saw no reason to worry about such matters, for there was little in the West to attract the businessman. Yet the westward movement was continuous, as it would be throughout the 19th century, and as the War of 1812 faded into the past, new thousands found homes beyond the mountains. The new Westerners were eager to trade, and Eastern businessmen began to realize that opportunity did not lie only in the Atlantic Ocean. Just beyond the mountain passes lay timber, pelts, salt, lead, hogs, cattle, and grain. And almost like the Indians, the white Westerners would take New England gewgaws and small manufactures in exchange.

The earliest solution to the problem of land transportation was the turnpike, or improved road. By 1794 the Lancaster Turnpike, running from Philadelphia to Lancaster in Pennsylvania, had become the model for hundreds like it. Aside from its crushed-stone surface, which made it an "all-weather" road, its easy 4% grade, and its fine bridges, the road had another distinctive feature: It was privately constructed. This was necessary because neither the state nor the federal government had exhibited much interest in highway building. In the case of the Lancaster Turnpike, built at a cost of $465,000, the state cooperated to the extent of granting the company the authority to condemn the necessary right-of-way. Then, after setting up toll gates seven miles apart along the road, the managers charged for the passage of people, animals, and vehicles, the last being assessed according to the width of their wheels. The Lancaster experiment was not a great success from a financial standpoint, but the idea appealed to Americans so much that by the time Albert Gallatin made his report on roads in 1808, he could write that in the state of New York alone there were 67 such companies, which were managing 900 miles of privately constructed road.

Impatiently the Westerners waited, vexed at conservative Eastern financiers, whose own roads were relatively good, and who were reluctant to invest their money in projects that might encourage westward migration and thereby increase the labor shortage in the Northeast. Pennsylvania, across whose territory many pioneers would have to travel, was at last moved to buy $100,000 worth of stock in a company that promised to extend the Lancaster Turnpike westward to Wheeling, on the Ohio River. This extension, the Cumberland (or National) Road was built at a cost of about $13,000 a mile, and after many difficulties, both legal and technical, it was finally completed in 1818. Ohioans showed their interest in the project by turning over a percentage of the sales from public lands in the new state to secure a connection with the Atlantic Ocean. Happy, too, were the merchants of Baltimore and Philadelphia, who hoped that their respective cities would now emerge as the commercial leaders of the seaboard.

The Cumberland Road was warmly

In 1821, even in winter, stages went from Providence to Worcester in a day, for $3.

welcomed by those who wished to trade or travel. Over it, and its counterparts that soon sprang up, flowed all kinds of traffic from private carriages to the crudest carts. Newly formed stagecoach lines called by such names as the June Bug Line, the Pioneer Line, and the National Line did a flourishing business. That the new means of travel was not the ultimate in comfort is suggested by the name of the one called the Shake Gut Line. Despite such discomforts, passengers were delighted that they could bump across the land at an average speed of close to six miles an hour and that the Ohio River was now only $17.25 away from Baltimore.

Freighters made equally good use of the Lancaster-Cumberland Road. As early as 1817, a year before the road to Wheeling was finished, one contemporary wrote that 12,000 wagons had arrived at Pittsburgh from Baltimore and Philadelphia. The highway made possible a new kind of triangular trade by which enterprising merchants could send selected goods overland to the headwaters of the Ohio, raft them down as far as New Orleans or sell them along the way, and then proceed by ship back to the East Coast to start the process all over again.

New equipment matched the new roads. The Conestoga wagon soon became the most famous freight vehicle on the turnpike. Its boatlike shape, with each end about a foot higher than the middle to make it more maneuverable on rough terrain, made it unique. Topped with canvas supported by huge bows, it was the

A crowd watches as this stagecoach, pulled by 10 horses and called the Seventy Six, leaves with its overflow of three passengers seated on the top.

prototype of the prairie schooner soon to be so widely known west of the Missouri River. These broad-wheeled wagons, pulled by six-horse teams, carried enormous loads.

In addition to their contribution to transportation, the Conestoga wagons left a social note on the American scene. The drivers, a tough, rough-housing breed, found that along with profanity one of the necessities of their calling was a good cigar. They complained so about the high price of cigars that an enterprising individual devised a smaller, but cheaper and more potent, product. They were so widely used by the teamsters that they became known as Conestogies, later shortened to "stogies."

One of the most notable results of such improved transportation facil-

ities to the west side of the mountains was the decline in freight rates. In 1817 it cost $9.50 to ship 100 pounds of freight from Pittsburgh to Phila-delphia. Within a year that cost fell to $6.50. But rates were still high for bulkier products. The charge of $13 a barrel for hauling flour over the same distance kept the volume low for some time to come. While the turnpike was a satisfactory solution to the problem of passenger and small-freight haul-age, another answer had to be found for heavier and larger items. The solu-tion was the canal.

Nautical teamsters

As merchants and freighters con-templated ways of hauling great quantities, they rediscovered a fact known for centuries: Water transpor-

tation was the cheapest. It was estimated that four horses could pull a ton 12 miles a day over an ordinary road and 18 miles over a good turnpike, but they could haul 100 tons 24 miles by water in the same period. Canals—man-made waterways—were an ancient conception. They appeared to be the answer to interior America's growing transportation needs.

The attraction to canals was more than taproom talk. City people around the fine harbor of New York regarded them with a sense of urgency. By 1818 Baltimore and Philadelphia, now connected to the Ohio River by turnpike, threatened to eclipse New York as a commercial center. Already the steamboat was becoming a practicality on Western waters. Steam would make a two-way street out of the

Mississippi-Ohio River system, and then the road eastward from Pittsburgh would be clogged with an even greater traffic. Provincial as well as metropolitan New Yorkers, who had assumed a take-it-or-leave-it attitude about the West, now awoke to the facts of economic life, and soon they embarked upon a crash program of canal building.

By 1817 the New York legislature was persuaded to pass legislation that made possible construction of the Erie Canal. Paced by the enthusiasm of New York Governor DeWitt Clinton, and under the direction of two lawyers who practiced engineering on

433

There was a canal through Virginia's Dismal Swamp by 1805, with lumber its main commodity, but the artist imagined the kind of craft that traveled it.

the side, the amateur canal builders went to work. In what turned out to be a school for canal engineers, the project was completed with remarkable speed, considering that it was done largely by hand and by horse. In 1825 the canal's 363 miles between Buffalo and Albany were opened to traffic. A contemporary writer observed, "They have built the longest canal in the world in the least time, with the least experience, for the least money, and to the greatest public benefit." Within 25 years the writer might have added another significant fact: In that short time the canal's tolls paid for its construction several times over.

Long before that, other Americans had seen the tremendous possibilities of canals. Once a connection between the Atlantic Ocean and the Great Lakes was assured, Midwestern promoters began to build a whole network of canals between those inland oceans and the Ohio River. Now farmers from New York to Illinois watched teams of stocky horses plodding canal towpaths, tugging along a new breed of sailors and their cargoes. While canal transportation was designed primarily to haul heavy freight, it was widely used by passengers. On the Erie Canal, packet boats moved along at four miles an hour, charging fares of 3¢ to 4¢ a mile, for which passengers received not only bed and board, but a degree of comfort denied by closely packed stagecoaches.

The freshly cut ditches and the brightly colored boats that glided along them meant a great deal to inland communities. Not only could the necessaries of life be brought in more cheaply, but for the first time it was feasible to ship out large quantities of agricultural produce. The effect was dual: Western farmers could get away from their homespun industries to a degree that permitted them to specialize agriculturally and to deal in a cash economy; and further, rising New England manufacturing centers could both find a market for their wares and rely upon a supply of Western farm products for their tables.

Advanced transportation facilities, while important to the nation at large, were particularly welcomed by the various sections. Westerners watched with delight as falling freight rates drove down the price of goods brought in, and at the same time gave them a greater share of the profits when they sold their produce. Real-estate and personal-property values in Ohio rose much faster in counties having canals than in those not served by them.

Western cities grew rapidly, thanks to these improvements. Cleveland, for example, saw its population grow fiftyfold in the second quarter of the 19th century. Toledo, Chicago, Milwaukee, and Detroit also experienced boom times as immigrants poured in, eager to find farms.

In the Northeast, the effect of Western agricultural competition brought about specialization in dairy and truck farming to take advantage of nearby expanding markets in the growing Eastern cities. From a long-range point of view, the canals thus provided an important economic link connecting interdependent regions, the Northeast and the Midwest. Also, the specialization now made possible in each section tended to break down antagonisms Westerners had harbored against their Eastern brethren for decades. As the American Civil War approached, this became more and more important.

The age of steam

Canals solved some of the problems of transporting freight that turnpikes could not, but they were by no means the final answer. Aside from being expensive to build, and in rough country nearly impossible to construct, they were often frozen into uselessness during the winter months. When the canals were thus closed, and roads made impassable by long stretches of bad weather, huge amounts of produce would pile up in warehouses to await the coming of spring. To carry heavy freight long distances at relatively low rates and in all kinds of weather, transportation men turned to a new instrument the railroad.

Considering American ingenuity and the great need for transportation facilities, it is surprising that the railroad was not developed earlier. Its essential elements were well known before 1800 in England, where stationary steam engines were used to haul coal cars out of the mines. Yet even the Eastern regions of the United States, with available money and a traffic potential, did little in railroading before the 1830s. They probably would have delayed even longer had

not the whip of necessity lashed them into action. New England glumly watched New York reap huge rewards from the Erie Canal. The Pennsylvanians tried to duplicate the feat by building enormously expensive canal systems. Southerners looked on, jealous of the busy Northerners but thwarted by the great mountains that reared up to confound even prospective canal builders. The railroad—new-fangled, dangerous and possibly impractical—appeared to be a risky but necessary venture.

During 1830 and 1831 the legislature of Massachusetts chartered three railroads. All of them were completed in five years and all of them, of course,

radiated from Boston. By 1842 rail connections between Boston and Albany, on the Erie Canal, were completed, with the aid of funds from nervous New England capitalists and almost $4,000,000 from the state of Massachusetts. Between 1830 and 1850 almost 3,000 miles of railroad were constructed in New England. By the end of that period Yankee manufactures were being carried all the way to the Great Lakes by rail. Indirectly, DeWitt Clinton may be credited for loosening a number of tightly strung Puritan purses. It was bet or get out of the game.

The South accepted the railroad much more readily but for the same reason—fear of commercial rivals. In South Carolina the city fathers of Charleston watched anxiously as New Orleans and even Savannah prospered. In 1828 Charleston's Chamber of Commerce secured a charter for a railroad to run from that city to Hamburg, on the Savannah River opposite Augusta, Georgia. The road, 136 miles in length, was projected for the purpose of capturing some of Savannah's trade. When it was completed, in 1833, it was the world's longest railroad. By no means satisfied, the

This 1830 locomotive, the second made in the United States, ran between Charleston and Hamburg. On this trip it carried a band to entertain its few passengers.

Carolinians dreamed of the day they could tap the Ohio River by rail and become a great international trading center, exporting Midwestern cereals and livestock. Neighboring Georgians saw the point, and decided to build west to capture frontier traffic. They constructed the Western & Atlantic, which was state owned and operated. It was 1851 before this road reached Chattanooga and finally Memphis, but despite many delays it still was the first to tap the South's western back country.

The early railroads were crude and certainly dangerous contraptions. So feeble were the power units that occasionally a horse was carried along as a "spare" in case of difficulties. Some roads stored their locomotives during the winter and used horses, to insure service. The track, timbers laid end to end and covered with narrow straps of thin metal, varied in gauge

from four to six feet. On these primitive roads one might find a half-dozen different gauges in the same region, a condition that prevented through lines from developing. Signal systems were in their infancy, and through their failure, or the tendency of the strap-iron rails to come loose and knife through coach floors, a number of bad accidents occurred.

Atop all these problems lay a great hostility toward the railroads on the part of those who had invested heavily in canal bonds, and of farmers and tavern operators who made money by feeding stagecoach horses and passengers along the turnpikes. These vested interests were not without influence. In 1833, when the Utica & Schenectady Railroad applied for a charter, the New York legislature stipulated that nothing but passengers and baggage could be carried by rail. Later the legislators relented and allowed the carriage of freight, provided the railroad paid the state canal fund the amount of money it would have collected in fees had the goods gone by canal boat. Such opposition was gradually overcome by the demonstrated superiority of the railroad and the public's enthusiastic reception of it.

In the West, much of which was not served by either canals or improved highways, there was no prejudice against the rail lines, but they suffered from other limitations. The new land was characterized by a sparse and widely spread population, an absence of large cities, chronic lack of capital, and a traditional animosity toward the Eastern investing class that might be induced to sink money into rail ventures. Nevertheless, the railroad was the answer to the West's problems, and despite all these difficulties the new form of transportation came to that region.

The task of penetrating the great Appalachian Range with rail lines was accomplished largely during the late 1840s and early 1850s. In view of the existing engineering knowledge and the available facilities, the feat in many respects was more significant than the achievements of those who later crossed the Sierras and Rockies with their construction crews. The New York & Erie reached the Great Lakes by 1851, the same year the Western & Atlantic entered Chattanooga. The Baltimore & Ohio was completed in 1852, and within another year the New York Central road was organized.

After some organizational fumbling, and experiments in state construction, railroad building was entrusted to the hands of private enterprise. Flinty-eyed entrepreneurs made the most of their opportunities. However, they did not do it without help. Rather early the roads became the accepted carriers of mail and troops, and the subsidies granted them lent much-needed financial support. Far more important aid came from government grants of land. When, in 1850, the Illinois Central was given alternate sections of land on each side of its route, a practice was established that later would make possible the construction of transcontinental lines.

Before the time of the Civil War the government had handed out about 32,000,000 acres for this purpose.

Empire builders on rails

The turnpikes, canals, and railroads together supplied the essential transportation links for the development of American manufacture and commerce. Of the three, the railroad came to be the most important because of its efficiency and greater adaptability. Its advantages over the turnpike were obvious, and it could penetrate new country inaccessible to canals, a factor that after 1860 overcame the waterways.

New states were not long in taking advantage of the cheaper means of travel. As early as 1845 the Michigan state legislature provided funds to pay an agent, stationed in New York, for sending on any immigrants he could find. That state also published thousands of pamphlets for distribution throughout Europe, hoping to attract land-hungry farmers. Neighboring Wisconsin followed a similar course, fearful that its opportunities might go unnoticed. When Illinois failed to join the competition, the Illinois Central Railroad took up the cause and embarked upon the greatest advertising campaign of that day. Its pamphlets were sent to thousands of post offices, with requests to tack them up on a convenient wall. Railroad advertising appeared in all Eastern port-city newspapers and in those of every little agricultural community sus-

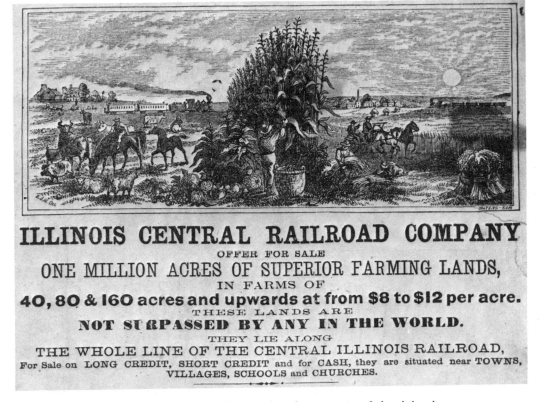

ILLINOIS CENTRAL RAILROAD COMPANY
OFFER FOR SALE
ONE MILLION ACRES OF SUPERIOR FARMING LANDS,
IN FARMS OF
40, 80 & 160 acres and upwards at from $8 to $12 per acre.
THESE LANDS ARE
NOT SURPASSED BY ANY IN THE WORLD.
THEY LIE ALONG
THE WHOLE LINE OF THE CENTRAL ILLINOIS RAILROAD,
For Sale on LONG CREDIT, SHORT CREDIT and for CASH, they are situated near TOWNS, VILLAGES, SCHOOLS and CHURCHES.

The Illinois Central was the first railroad to use its federal land grants to lure settlers onto its line and out to land that ran along its right of way.

pected of having discontented farmers. The company was eager to utilize the lands granted it, both for cash profit and to populate its route with prospective customers. In so doing, it set a pattern followed by a majority of the trans-Mississippi roads a few years later.

By the 1850s American growth was a matter of surprised comment, even among Americans. In the West, the fastest-growing part of the nation, it was the railroad that was of prime importance in this development. It helped to populate the new country, particularly its more remote parts.

It provided America with a whole new industry—railroading itself. The business of manufacturing locomotives, cars, rails, and equipment was important to a growing steel industry. The railroad's ability to transport passengers and all kinds of freight rapidly gave older sections, such as New England, new industrial opportunities, while it allowed Western agriculture to specialize as it never had before. Even in its infancy it was predicted that the railroad would become the economic bloodstream of America, a forecast that has abundantly been fulfilled.

MAIN TEXT CONTINUES IN VOLUME 6

It was the cotton kingdom, ruled by landowning whites but based upon the hard labor of black slaves, that Eli Whitney's revolutionary invention brought strongly into existence. This Currier and Ives print portrays an unusually bountiful cotton harvest in full swing.

Eli Whitney:
Nemesis of the South

A SPECIAL CONTRIBUTION BY
ARNOLD WHITRIDGE

A New England schoolteacher invented the cotton gin that revolutionized the South, and then he laid the foundations for the North's industrial power that would conquer it.

Any American who ruminates about the origins of the Civil War—and that should mean not only professional historians but everyone in the United States, North and South, who has ever been spellbound by the story of his country—will find himself sooner or later confronted by an ingenious contraption for removing seeds from the cotton boll, known as the cotton gin.

This device, invented by Eli Whitney, a totally unknown young man just out of Yale College, changed the whole pattern of cotton production. No invention ever answered a more pressing need.

Immediately after graduating from Yale in 1792, Whitney was engaged as a private tutor for a family in Georgia. On his way to take up his post, he made the acquaintance of Mrs. Nathanael Greene, widow of the Revolutionary general, who was returning to Savannah after spending the summer in the North. An invitation to stay at Mrs. Greene's plantation, all the more welcome when he discovered that his prospective employer had hired another man in his place, brought him into contact with the cotton aristocracy of the neighborhood. Whitney soon endeared himself to his

hostess by his extraordinary "handiness." There was nothing this big, rambling man with the extraordinary deft fingers could not make or mend.

As a boy on the farm, the oldest of five children, he had always preferred puttering around his father's metalworking shop to doing the farm chores. He was born in Westboro, Massachusetts, in 1765, the year of the Stamp Act. By the time he was grown, the exciting days of the Revolution were over, and the farmers of Massachusetts were learning to their amazement that independence and prosperity did not necessarily go hand in hand. Some of them, discouraged by debts they could not pay, joined Shays' Rebellion against the state government, but Eli Whitney stuck to the farm and eked out the family income by manufacturing nails, even hiring a helper to fill his orders. When the demand for nails slacked off, he turned to making hatpins and walking canes. Neighbors got into the habit of looking up Eli whenever they needed anything repaired. For one of them he even made a violin, which was said to have produced "tolerable good music."

At the age of 18, it came home to him that he needed a college degree if he was ever to be anything more than a clever mechanic. The family was not sympathetic: By the time he had prepared himself for college, he would be too old, and besides, they could not afford it. Eli listened to all their complaints and then disregarded them. He taught school for three winters, finally won his father's consent, and was admitted to Yale in 1789, when he was 23.

When Whitney was painted in 1822, three years before his death, by Samuel F. B. Morse, he had little idea of the effect of his inventions.

Yale graduate who was staying with her. They were bemoaning the fact that there was no quick, practical way of separating short-staple cotton from its seed. It took a slave 10 hours to separate one pound of lint from three pounds of the small, tough seeds. Under those conditions, no one in the South could afford to grow cotton, and yet in other parts of the world, cotton was becoming a semiprecious commodity. "Gentlemen," said Mrs. Greene, "tell your troubles to Mr. Whitney. He can make anything."

Mr. Whitney could and did. Within two weeks he had produced a model of the cotton gin, an ingenious device that was destined to have an ultimately disastrous effect upon the people it enriched. The cotton was dragged through a wire screen by means of toothed cylinders revolving toward each other. A revolving brush cleaned the cylinders, and the seeds fell into another compartment. A later model, run by water power, could produce 300 to 1,000 pounds a day.

Whitney wrote to his father that he hoped to keep his invention a "profound secret," but word of it spread so quickly that long before he could get to Washington and take out a patent, his workshop had been broken into and his machine examined. The interlopers discovered that the gin was easy to copy, and because it was, cotton was planted on a scale never dreamed of before. In 1792, the United States was exporting only 138,000 pounds. Two years later, that figure had risen to 1,601,000. Never had any invention made such an immediate impression upon society, abroad as well as at home.

In England, the invention of spinning frames and power looms had created a demand that could be filled only from the Southern states. Supplies from the Levant, from Guiana, and from the West Indies, which had met nearly all needs down to 1794, fell into the background as the export of American slave-grown and mechanically ginned cotton suddenly began to climb. By the end of the first quarter of the 19th century, America was shipping to Liverpool more than three-quarters of all the cotton used in the United

He was not a brilliant student, but when the Reverend Ezra Stiles, president of Yale, was asked to recommend a suitable person for a private tutor out of the graduating class of 1792, Whitney was the one he chose.

Evidently Mrs. Greene in Savannah had faith in him, too, and when a party of her friends, officers who had served under General Greene in the Revolution, were discussing the deplorable state of agriculture in their neighborhood, she referred them to the young

444

Kingdom. Eli Whitney had conjured up an army of 450,000 cotton workers in England. Ten thousand power looms and 240,000 hand looms secured the cotton planters against the danger of a glutted market.

The existence of this market and being able to supply it with ease and profit made cotton planting the greatest industry in the South. The Louisiana Purchase had opened to slave-holding settlement and culture a vast domain of the richest soil on earth in a region peculiarly adapted to the expanding production of cotton. As production grew, so did the value of a slave. By 1825, when cotton was selling at 15¢ a pound, a good black field hand who 20 years earlier had been worth only $500 would often bring $1,500 on a New Orleans auction block.

The phenomenal success of the cotton industry, for which Eli Whitney was directly responsible, gave birth in the South to an entirely new conception of slavery. In the early days of the Republic, the most thoughtful Southerners, including Washington and Jefferson, had deprecated slavery as an evil that must eventually be swept away. No one denied that slavery was morally wrong and a menace to the country. Almost every Virginian hoped to make real the words of his state's bill of rights, "that all men are by nature equally free and independent." As the Marquis de Chastellux, a major general in Rochambeau's army in America during the Revolution, wrote,

"They are constantly talking of abolishing slavery, and of contriving some other means of cultivating their estates."

Such ideas gradually came to be regarded as old-fashioned. What, asked Daniel Webster in 1850, had created the new feeling in favor of slavery in the South, so that it became an institution to be cherished—"no evil, no scourge, but a great religious, social and moral blessing? I suppose this is owing to the rapid growth and sudden extension of the cotton plantations of the South."

The doctrine that cotton was king, and that all other interests in the nation would bow before it, had permeated the whole South by the middle of the century. Few of the Northerners who scoffed at this doctrine remembered that it was a Northern inventor who gave slavery its new lease on life. It was hard to protest against a system upon which the whole prosperity of one section of the country seemed to hinge. Unwittingly, Eli Whitney had set in motion an undercurrent against the notions of equality and freedom. He himself made nothing out of his cotton gin, but he was nonetheless the founder of the cotton empire—an empire that everybody believed would inevitably collapse if the underpinning of slavery were removed.

The cotton gin, like many other inventions, turned out to be so valuable to the world as to be worthless to its inventor. The government could offer Whitney no protection

Whitney's cotton gin was the most notable of America's early contributions to the Industrial Revolution. This model is one of several made by Whitney in applying for a patent. He filed his first application in 1793 with Thomas Jefferson, who was then Secretary of State and head of the Patent Office, but he never received full protection for his invention.

The reproductions above are from an old advertisement for Whitney's gun factory, where he filled his first government contract in 1798.

against the infringement of patent rights. The suits he brought were tried before juries of the very men who were breaking the patents.

Unable to make a living out of the cotton gin, Whitney turned his back on the South. He settled in New Haven and determined to devote himself to the production of something profitable—something that could not easily be copied and appropriated by others. In 1798, disturbed by the danger of war with France, he wrote to Oliver Wolcott, Secretary of the Treasury, offering to manufacture "ten or fifteen thousand Stand of Arms." By "stand of arms" was meant the complete arms necessary to equip a soldier—the musket, bayonet, ramrod, wiper, and screw driver.

After some haggling, the offer was accepted. Whitney journeyed down to Washington and returned to New Haven with a contract in his pocket for 10,000 muskets, selling for $13.40 each, to be delivered within two years. He proposed to manufacture these muskets on a new principle—the principle of interchangeable parts.

Here was a man who as early as 1798 could visualize the government's need of a constant supply of firearms, who could devise methods of production that would guarantee such a supply, and who, handicapped by the lack of a machine that would enable workmen to cut metal according to pattern, proceeded to invent one that has remained unchanged in principle for more than a century and a half. This milling machine, as it was called, was the cornerstone of his new system of interchangeable parts. Life in America had produced plenty of mechanics, particularly in New England, but few craftsmen. What Whitney did was to substitute for the skill of the craftsman the uniformity of the machine.

Foreigners have often observed as one of the characteristics of American industry that we build from the top down rather than from the ground up. Eli Whitney did not start with a few workmen and then gradually expand. He tooled up first. Before a single workman walked into his factory, he designed and built all the machinery he would need for his method of production. At the same time he proved himself a practical businessman as well as an inventor. He understood how to obtain contracts, finance their execution, and provide funds for future expansion.

The importance of what Whitney was doing did not readily penetrate the official mind.

His friend Wolcott had been replaced in the Treasury by Samuel Dexter, a Massachusetts lawyer, who instinctively distrusted theories not sanctioned by experience. Whitney's methods seemed to him unorthodox. As if to justify his suspicions, Whitney was soon running behind on his schedule of deliveries. In the first year, only 500 guns were produced instead of the stipulated 4,000.

Fortunately the new President, Thomas Jefferson, was blessed with a receptive, ranging mind. The idea of interchangeable parts was already familiar to him. In 1785, while minister to France, he had visited the workshop of a Monsieur LeBlanc, who was making muskets on exactly that principle. Jefferson himself had put together the parts of 50 locks, "taking pieces at hazard as they came to hand." He was so impressed by this new method of manufacture that he suggested bringing LeBlanc over to America, but the government was not interested in newfangled techniques. Nor indeed was the French government, which probably distrusted any invention that might lead to unemployment.

In England, too, other men had anticipated Whitney. Joseph Bramah, the great machine designer, and Marc Brunel, a young French Royalist officer who had been driven out of his country during the Revolution, had manufactured pulley blocks with interchangeable parts for the British navy, but it was left to an American to apply the process to mass production and put it to the service of mankind.

Whitney himself probably never realized how far his system would reach. The new technique that had been used for the manufacture of firearms was soon found to be no less applicable to other industries. The Connecticut clockmakers began making brass clocks instead of wooden clocks, as soon as the advantages of interchangeable parts were recognized. Elias Howe and Isaac Singer followed with the sewing machine, and before the outbreak of the Civil War, Cyrus McCormick and his rivals were producing the harvesters and reapers that rolled back the frontier and revolutionized farming the world over.

For these inventions and a hundred others,

Eli Whitney paved the way. The successful application of his theory proved a landmark in the over-all growth of American mass production. In Europe, however, where there was no shortage of skilled labor, the idea made slow progress. It caught on only in gunmaking, where the advantages were too obvious to be ignored. By the middle of the 19th century, nearly every government in Europe was supplied with American gunmaking machinery.

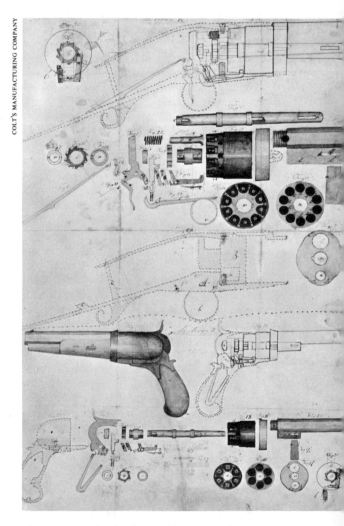

COLT'S MANUFACTURING COMPANY

The system of interchangeable parts, devised by Whitney and carried on by Samuel Colt in Whitney's armory, is shown in this 1853 illustration of Colt's first patent for his firearms.

In the Southern states, the planters who had profited so enormously from the cotton gin paid no attention to the increasing tempo of industrial activity in the North. South Carolina paid $50,000 to Whitney as a belated acknowledgment of what society owed him, but no one in the South seemed aware of the new techniques in manufacture that he evolved—techniques of which the seceding states were soon to find themselves desperately in need. Conditions of labor, soil, and climate had produced a static society that refused to accept the implications of the 19th century.

It is one of the ironies of history that the man who inadvertently contributed to the downfall of the South by his invention of the cotton gin should also have blazed the trail leading to the technological supremacy of the North. The loss of the will to fight in the closing days of the Confederacy can be traced in large part to the feeling that the South had reached the limit of its resources, whereas in the North every deficiency in equipment could always be made good.

No distinction can be made between the Union and the Confederate soldier in their inherent fighting ability, but in the quantity as well as the quality of their equipment the advantage was all with the Northerner. Although the extraordinarily resourceful General Josiah Gorgas, Confederate chief of ordnance, managed to keep his armies supplied with the necessary weapons and munitions up to the very end of the war, even he could not keep pace with the inventiveness and the productivity of Northern arsenals and factories. More than once, a single Union regiment, armed with breech-loading rifles, held in check a whole brigade armed with the ordinary musket. As one Confederate soldier put it, "It's no use for us to fight you'uns with that kind of gun."

The disparity in clothing and equipment was even more marked than the disparity in weapons. The Southern soldier had to find most of his own equipment, whereas the Northerner was supplied by the government. If the Union soldier faced privation, as he often did, it was the fault of shady contractors and incompetent quartermasters. The New England factories were turning out all the uniforms, the boots, and the varied accouterments he could possibly need.

The Civil War was the first of the truly modern wars, in which the industrial potential of a nation forms the foundation on which all military plans and achievements must ultimately be built. Given that situation, the advantage was all with the North.

Before the war even began, William Tecumseh Sherman warned a Southern friend that a purely agricultural region like the South could not hope to win against a nation of mechanics. "You are bound to fail," he said, and events bore him out. As the war went on, the entire Southern economy came under intolerable strain. In the end, it simply became impossible for the Confederacy to carry the burden any longer.

On the other hand, the North could produce, in almost any required volume, the infinite variety and number of goods needed to support a nation at war. For this technique it was, to a large extent, indebted to Eli Whitney.

Whitney died in 1825, long before the "irrepressible conflict" had cast its shadow over American history. He himself was unaware of the part he had played in the expansion of slavery, just as he was unaware of the mighty industrial forces he had set in motion. He had invented the cotton gin and he had manufactured muskets on a new system for a war against France that never materialized, but by those two achievements he had affected the whole course of American history. By the first he riveted slavery on the South and thus created a tension between the two sections of the country that could be resolved only by war. And by the second he gave an impetus to the mass production of inexpensive goods that has created what the world knows as the American standard of living, and that has reunited us, with all the differences in our backgrounds, into an amazingly homogeneous nation.

Arnold Whitridge has been Master of Calhoun College, Yale University, and professor in the Department of History, Arts, and Letters. His most recent book is No Compromise! *(1960).*

Volume 5

ENCYCLOPEDIC SECTION

The two-page reference guide below lists the entries by categories. The entries in this section supplement the subject matter covered in the text of this volume. A **cross-reference** (*see*) means that a separate entry appears elsewhere in this section. However, certain important persons and events mentioned here have individual entries in the Encyclopedic Section of another volume. Consult the Index in Volume 18.

AMERICAN STATESMEN AND POLITICIANS

John Quincy Adams
William Taylor Barry
Thomas Hart Benton
Francis P. Blair
John C. Calhoun
Henry Clay
DeWitt Clinton
William Crawford
Richard Henry Dana
John Henry Eaton
Thomas Ewing
John Forsyth
Felix Grundy
William Henry Harrison
Robert Hayne

Philip Hone
Andrew Jackson
Richard M. Johnson
Amos Kendall
William B. Lewis
Louis McLane
Horace Mann
John Marshall
Peter Buell Porter
John Randolph
Richard Rush
James Tallmadge
Roger Taney
Jesse Thomas
Martin Van Buren
William Wirt

BUILDING A NEW NATION

canals
Conestoga wagon
Cotton Kingdom
Cumberland Road
Erie Canal

immigration
Industrial Revolution
Lancaster Turnpike
railroads
steamboats

FINANCE AND FINANCIERS

Nicholas Biddle
Panic of 1819
Panic of 1837

George Peabody
Second Bank of the United States
Specie Circular

FOREIGN RELATIONS

Adams-Onis Treaty
Alexander I (Russia)
Arbuthnot-Ambrister Affair
Sir Charles Bagot (Great Britain)
George Canning (Great Britain)
Convention of 1818
Monroe Doctrine
Richard Rush
Rush-Bagot Agreement

INDIANS

Cherokees
Seminoles
Sequoyah
Trail of Tears
Samuel A. Worcester
Worcester vs. Georgia

INVENTORS AND INDUSTRIALISTS

Joseph Bramah
Moses Brown
Sir Marc Brunel
Samuel Colt
Peter Cooper
Eleuthere Irenee du Pont
Oliver Evans
Charles Goodyear
Elias Howe
Amos Kendall
Cyrus McCormick
Samuel F. B. Morse
Nathaniel Palmer
Isaac M. Singer
Samuel Slater
Charles Thurber
Eli Whitney

POLITICAL DEVELOPMENTS

Amistad Case
Brown vs. Maryland
Clay Compromise Tariff
Cohens vs. Virginia
Compromise of 1833
Force Bill
gag rule
Gibbons vs. Ogden
McCulloch vs. Maryland
Marbury vs. Madison
Missouri Compromise
Ordinance of Nullification
political parties
spoils system
Tariff of Abominations
Tariff of 1828
Twelfth Amendment
Webster-Hayne Debate

THE PRESIDENCY

John Quincy Adams
Peggy Eaton
William Henry Harrison
Andrew Jackson
Richard M. Johnson
spoils system
Twelfth Amendment
Martin Van Buren

THOUGHT AND CULTURE

Louis Agassiz
John James Audubon
Thomas Hart Benton
George Caleb Bingham
Carl Bodmer
Moses Brown
Alonzo Chappel
Peter Cooper
Richard Henry Dana
Joel Tanner Hart
Nathaniel Hawthorne
Washington Irving
John Lewis Krimmel
Benjamin Latrobe
Horace Mann
Harriet Martineau
John Neagle
Duncan Phyfe
Henry Rutgers
Felix Achille Saint-Aulaire
Margaret Bayard Smith
Alexis de Tocqueville
Mason Locke Weems
William Wirt

A

ADAMS, John Quincy (1767–1848). Adams, the sixth President of the United States, and his father, John Adams (1735–1826), were the only two non-Virginian Chief Executives in the first 40 years of the American Republic. John Quincy Adams was also the only son of a President to reach that office himself. Of the first seven Presidents, only the Adamses were denied reelection. Born in Braintree (now Quincy), Massachusetts, young John Quincy gained his first diplomatic experience while in Europe (1778–1783) with his father during the Revolution. He studied on the Continent and served as secretary to the American minister to Russia. Adams graduated from Harvard College in 1787 and became a lawyer three years later. After serving as American minister to the Netherlands (1794–1796) and as minister to Prussia (1797–1801), he was elected to the Senate in 1803.

John Quincy Adams

Adams was a Federalist but often did not back his party's policies. For example, as an alternative to war with Britain or France, he supported the Embargo Act of 1807, which was opposed by the Federalists and which virtually ended American commerce with other nations. Because of this stand, Adams lost his Senate seat in 1808. For the rest of his career, he ignored party affiliation. Returning to the diplomatic service, Adams became minister to Russia (1809–1814) and negotiated favorable commercial treaties with that nation (*see* **Alexander I**). In 1814, he played an important role in writing the Peace of Ghent with Britain, which officially ended the War of 1812. Adams then served as minister to Britain, before becoming Secretary of State in 1817. In this position he made some of his greatest contributions to the nation. He negotiated the **Adams-Onis Treaty** (*see*) of 1819, by which Spain ceded East and West Florida to the United States, and he persuaded President James Monroe (1758–1831) to formulate the **Monroe Doctrine** (*see*) in 1823. Adams ran for President in 1824 against three other candidates— **Andrew Jackson, William Crawford,** and **Henry Clay** (*see all*). He received fewer electoral votes than Jackson, but no candidate received a majority and the election was decided by the House of Representatives. Adams was selected after Clay threw his support to him. During his term in office (1825–1829), Adams received little public support for his policies. He attempted many internal improvements in the government, but his administration was generally ineffective. He was subsequently defeated for reelection by Jackson in 1828. Adams later served almost 17 years in the House of Representatives (1831–1848). Because he advocated freedom of speech, he bitterly opposed the **gag rule** (*see*) of 1836, which was designed to silence antislavery petitions. His opposition to this rule, which was finally repealed in 1844, firmly identified him as an opponent of slavery. Adams suffered a stroke while serving in the House and died on February 23, 1848, in the Capitol.

ADAMS–ONIS TREATY. Under the terms of the Adams-Onis Treaty in 1819, Spain ceded the territory known as the Floridas to the United States. The treaty, which is sometimes called the Transcontinental Treaty, was named after the two men who negotiated it—American Secretary of State **John Quincy Adams** (*see*) and the Spanish minister to the United States, Luis de Onis (1769–1830). Prior to the agreement—which was signed on February 22, 1819, and ratified two years later—the United States and Spain had disputed the ownership of West Florida, which had been permanently occupied by American troops by 1814. When **Andrew Jackson** attacked the **Seminoles** (*see both*) in East Florida in 1818, Spain, weakened by wars in Europe and colonial uprisings in Latin America, was powerless to defend the Floridas. She was also worried about the vagueness of the boundary between the United States and Spanish Mexico. Spain feared that American troops would invade Spanish Mexico from the Louisiana Territory, which the United States had purchased from France in 1803. These considerations led Spain to accept the terms outlined by Adams. For $5,000,000—which the United States agreed to pay to Americans who held claims against the Spanish government—Spain ceded East Florida to the United States and renounced all claims to West Florida. Spain also agreed to a boundary between Mexico and the United States. This was to extend from the Gulf of Mexico northward and then westward along the banks of the Sabine, Red, and Arkansas Rivers, then west to the Pacific along the 42nd parallel (the southern border of present-day Oregon). By this treaty, the United States recognized—temporarily—Spanish claims to what are now Texas, New Mexico, Arizona, Colorado, Nevada, Utah, and California.

FOGG ART MUSEUM, HARVARD UNIVERSITY

Louis Agassiz

AGASSIZ, Louis (1807–1873). In addition to making important contributions in the fields of geology and zoology, Agassiz played a central role in awakening interest in the study of science in America. Born in Switzerland, Agassiz studied medicine and natural science in his native country and in Germany. He won acclaim for his researches on fish fossils and for his theory that vast-ranging geological formations were caused by the movement of gla-

ciers during the Ice Age. A brilliant lecturer and teacher, Agassiz accepted an appointment (1848–1873) at Harvard College, where he founded the Museum of Comparative Zoology. He conducted extensive zoological research throughout North and South America and published widely. The first four volumes of his projected 10-volume *Contributions to the Natural History of the United States* were completed by 1857. At the time of his death, Agassiz had significantly advanced the cause of scientific education in the United States.

ALEXANDER I (1777–1825). Although deeply involved in the wars and politics of Europe during and after the Napoleonic era, Czar Alexander I of Russia often turned his attention to the young republic of America. A major influence in his interest was **John Quincy Adams** (*see*). In 1809, the 32-year-old Adams was sent as minister to the Russian court at St. Petersburg to seek the czar's support for American neutrality at sea. At this time, Alexander was an ally of the French emperor Napoleon (1769–1821), who was at war with Britain. Adams favorably impressed the czar, who, the following year, arranged for the release of 52 American ships captured by Napoleon's ally Denmark. In defiance of an economic agreement with Napoleon, the czar also lifted restrictions on American ships in Russian waters. When the War of 1812 began, the czar offered to mediate. Adams quickly accepted his offer, but the British, convinced they were winning the war, refused it. Under the **Convention of 1818** (*see*), Alexander was asked to negotiate American claims against Britain for slaves captured during the

war. In 1821, Adams was Secretary of State when the czar attempted to extend the boundary of Russian-owned Alaska south to the 51st parallel, thus annexing present-day Oregon. Adams was instrumental in getting a statement against European colonization of the American continent included in the **Monroe Doctrine** (*see*). As a result of a treaty in 1824, the czar agreed not to press his claim. Although a proponent of reform early in his reign (1801–1825), Alexander increasingly became reactionary in domestic affairs following Napoleon's final defeat at Waterloo in 1815. He also was involved in a mystical sect, and after his death there were rumors that he had instead disappeared into Siberia as a religious hermit. His casket was opened in 1926 and found empty.

AMBRISTER, Robert. *See* **Arbuthnot-Ambrister Affair.**

AMISTAD **CASE.** This case resulted in the most important Supreme Court ruling on slavery up to 1841. Two years before, the Spanish ship *Amistad* was transporting 54 slaves from Africa. Off Cuba, they revolted, killing several members of the Spanish crew and making the survivors sail north. An American warship stopped the *Amistad* in Long Island Sound and brought the slaves to New London, Connecticut. The slaves were tried by a local federal court, which ordered them returned to Spain. The slaves' appeals eventually reached the Supreme Court in 1841. Southerners urged that the slaves be surrendered to Spain or else punished. Abolitionists, who wanted the slaves released, hired **John Quincy Adams** (*see*) to defend them. His legal defense was so persuasive that the Court overruled the lower courts and freed the slaves. Money was then raised to pay for the slaves' return voyage to Africa.

ARBUTHNOT, Alexander. *See* **Arbuthnot-Ambrister Affair.**

ARBUTHNOT–AMBRISTER AFFAIR. While leading federal troops against the **Seminoles** (*see*) in the Spanish colony of East Florida in 1818, the American general **Andrew Jackson** (*see*) captured, court-martialed, and executed two British subjects—Alexander Arbuthnot and Robert Ambrister. Arbuthnot, a Scottish trader, was accused of informing the Seminoles of American troop movements. Ambrister, an English trader, had allegedly incited Indian hostilities. The British press protested strongly, calling the executions murder and branding Jackson a ruffian. However, the British government officially ignored the affair. Congressman **Henry Clay** (*see*) demanded that Jackson be disciplined, as did Secretary of War **John C. Calhoun** (*see*). Generally, however, Americans supported Jackson's determination to establish military control in Florida, and President James Monroe (1758–1831) refused to take any action against him. Spain protested American aggression in her territory, but Jackson's invasion made it clear that the Spanish were unable to control Florida. Spain ceded the colony to the United States the following year (*see* **Adams-Onis Treaty**).

AUDUBON, John James (1785?–1851). A naturalist and artist whose illustrations are well-known the world over, Audubon traveled through the wilderness of North America drawing birds in their

Naturalist John James Audubon explored North America to study wildlife.

natural surroundings. Born in Haiti, Audubon was raised and educated in France. Early in 1804, he arrived in America and settled near Philadelphia, where he continued his lifelong study of birds. After moving to Kentucky about 1808, he tried several occupations but often neglected business to pursue his interest in natural history and to draw birds. He was bankrupt by 1819, was jailed briefly for debts, and subsequently decided to try to publish his pictures. Unable to interest an American publisher, he took his work to Britain in 1826. His classic, *The Birds of America,* was published there in serial form between 1827 and 1838. A friend helped Audubon with the scientific part of the related text, which was published separately in five volumes by 1839. Audubon devoted the remainder of his life to preparing a book about North American mammals. It was completed by his sons three years after his death. Critics disagree about the value of Audubon's paintings. Some argue that they are scientifically inaccurate. Others insist

that they seem too much like photographs. However, in the opinion of Baron Georges Cuvier (1769–1832), the great French naturalist, Audubon's drawings were "the most magnificent monument that art had ever raised to science."

B

BAGOT, Sir Charles (1781–1843). Bagot was the British minister to the United States from 1815 to 1820. In April, 1817, he negotiated the **Rush-Bagot Agreement** with **Richard Rush** (*see both*), America's acting Secretary of State. This agreement limited British and American naval armament on the Great Lakes. Bagot later served (1841–1843) as the governor-general of Canada.

BARRY, William Taylor (1785–1835). Grateful for Barry's aid in the Presidential campaign of 1828, **Andrew Jackson** (*see*) appointed him Postmaster General in 1829. However, Barry resigned in protest in 1835 after Congress had investigated charges of misuse of funds in his department. Barry, though cleared of any wrongdoing, denounced the inquiry as a political move to discredit Jackson. Born in Virginia, Barry went to Kentucky with his family as a youth. He was educated at the College of William and Mary and studied law at Transylvania College. He became an attorney and a leader in the Democratic Party in Kentucky. Barry served in the state legislature and later in the United States Senate (1815–1816). Elected lieutenant governor in 1821, he sought unsuccessfully to end the depression then sweeping Kentucky following the **Panic of 1819** (*see*). After serving as head of the federal Post Office, Barry was named minister to Spain by Jackson. However, he died on his way to his new post.

BENTON, Thomas Hart (1782–1858). Benton, a member of the United States Senate for 30 years, was a leader of the Democrats and an ardent supporter of **Andrew Jackson** (*see*). After practicing law and serving in the Tennessee senate, he moved in 1815 to Missouri, where, as a lawyer and newspaper editor, he advocated Missouri's admission to the Union as a slave state. He was elected to the first of five consecutive terms in the Senate in 1820 and became a spokesman for Western interests, an advocate of westward expansion, and a defender of "sound" money. To promote expansion westward, he supported the occupation of Oregon, exploration, a cross-country railroad, and trade with Mexico. In 1828, Benton supported Jackson for the Presidency, ending a 15-year feud with him that resulted from a tavern brawl during which Benton's brother Jesse was stabbed,

Thomas Hart Benton

Benton was thrown down a flight of stairs, and Jackson was shot in the leg by one of the Benton brothers. A "hard-money man," he supported Jackson's successful attack on the **Second Bank of the United States** (*see*) and was the author of Jackson's **Specie Circular** (*see*)—for which he became known as Old Bullion. Benton had come to favor gradual abolition, and his support of antislavery constitutions in several Western states cost him reelection in 1850. Before his death, he wrote a two-volume autobiography, *Thirty Years' View,* surveying the course of politics from 1820 to 1850, and a 15-volume *Abridgement of the Debates in Congress from 1789 to 1856,* both valuable guides to the politics of a growing America.

BIDDLE, Nicholas (1786–1844). Biddle was president of the **Second Bank of the United States** (*see*) when it was the center of a bitter controversy involving President **Andrew Jackson** (*see*). The son of a wealthy Philadelphia family, Biddle studied at both the University of Pennsylvania and the Col-

lege of New Jersey (now Princeton), from which he graduated at the age of 15 as valedictorian of his class. In 1804, he went abroad and later became secretary to James Monroe (1758–1831), who was then minister to Britain. Upon returning to America in 1807, Biddle joined a literary periodical and edited the notes taken on the famous cross-country Lewis and Clark expedition (1804–1806). In 1819, Monroe, now President, asked Biddle to serve on the board of directors of the Second Bank of the United States. As president of the bank (1823–1836), Biddle instituted sound fiscal policies to stabilize the national currency and combat inflation. President Jackson, who believed the bank was too powerful and favored the interests of wealthy Eastern merchants, vetoed in 1831 a bill to renew the bank's charter. After his reelection the following year, Jackson withdrew all federal deposits. Biddle later established the Bank of the United States of Pennsylvania, which went bankrupt in 1841. He was charged with fraud, tried, and acquitted. He died soon after, a ruined man.

BINGHAM, George Caleb (1811–1879). Bingham's reputation as an artist is based on his paintings of scenes of everyday life in present-day Missouri. Born in Virginia, Bingham moved to Missouri while young. He established studios at Jefferson City, St. Louis, and later at Kansas City. Although he earned his living painting portraits of well-to-do Missourians, Bingham won widespread acclaim for the realism and humor of his paintings of commonplace scenes. His famous "river life" series was begun in 1844 (*see p. 410*). Many of Bingham's pictures had political themes, and this interest was carried over into his own career. Bingham was elected to the Missouri legislature in 1848 and held other state offices.

BLAIR, Francis P. (1791–1876). An astute politician and a skilled journalist, Blair was an adviser to two Presidents and helped to found the Republican Party. Born in Virginia, Blair studied law but never practiced it. Instead, he worked on newspapers, becoming an editorial writer on the *Argus of Western America* after the War of 1812. A Jacksonian Democrat, Blair criticized the policies of **Henry Clay** (*see*) and this—in addition to his support of lower tariffs, cheap land for settlers, and the direct election of the President —attracted the attention of President **Andrew Jackson** (*see*). In 1830, Jackson asked Blair to edit a newspaper presenting the administration's point of view. Blair subsequently founded the Washington *Globe* in 1830. Four years later, he started the *Congressional Globe,* which later became the *Congressional Record.* Blair, a member of Jackson's so-called kitchen cabinet, wielded consid-

Francis P. Blair

erable influence over administration policies. After 1845, he became disillusioned with the proslavery policies of the Democratic Party and was one of the principal organizers of the Republican Party (*see* **political parties**). He campaigned in 1860 for Abraham Lincoln (1809–1865) and after Lincoln's election became one of his advisers. Today, the government maintains Blair House, his Washington home, as a residence for high-ranking official visitors to the capital.

BODMER, Carl (1809–1893). Bodmer's paintings, watercolors, and drawings of the American West in the early 1830s are among the most valuable graphic records of the frontier in those pioneer days. Born in Switzerland, Bodmer served as artist-illustrator to the Prussian prince Alexander Philip Maximilian of Wied (1782–1867) on his natural-science expedition to America (1832–1834). After arriving in Boston, they traveled to Indiana and St. Louis, Missouri. From there they followed the Missouri River to Fort McKenzie, near what is now Great Falls, Montana (*see p. 417*). They took the same route back to St. Louis and then returned to New York, visiting the **Erie Canal** (*see*) and Niagara Falls on the way. As they traveled, Maximilian collected specimens, studied the Indians, and kept detailed accounts of his findings. Bodmer painted and drew the landscapes, vegetation, animals, and Indians that they saw. On his return home, the prince published (1839–1841) an account of the expedition, *Travels in the Interior of North America,* which was illustrated with 81 colorplates of Bodmer's Western watercolors. A collection of diaries, documents, and other records of the expedition, including 427 of Bodmer's works, is now at the Joslyn Art Museum in Omaha, Nebraska.

BRAMAH, Joseph (1748–1814). An English engineer, Bramah invented the safety lock and hydraulic press that bear his name. In 1784, he took out a patent on his safety lock. The hydraulic or Bramah press was patented in 1795. In 1806, he devised a numerical printing machine for the Bank of England. Other inventions included planing machines and improvements in the steam engine. Many of Bramah's suggestions later led to inventions by others, among them screw propulsion for ships and the hydraulic transmission of power. His work laid the foundations for the inventions of **Eli Whitney** (*see*) and others during the **Industrial Revolution** (*see*) in America.

BROWN, Moses (1738–1836). A successful New England merchant, Brown financed in 1790 the construction of the first factory in America. Born in Rhode Island, Brown was a member (1764–1771) of the colonial assembly and in 1774 freed his slaves and helped to found the Rhode Island Abolition Society. By 1789, Brown had begun experimenting with hand-operated cotton-spinning machinery. Upon learning that machinery of this type had been developed on a larger scale in England, he wrote to **Samuel Slater** (*see*), who had recently come to America, having memorized the plans for water-powered machinery to manufacture cotton cloth. With Brown's financial backing, Slater built a waterpowered cotton mill at Pawtucket, Rhode Island (*see pp. 380–381*). The venture was a financial success. Brown contributed much of the money he made to education. As a result of his generous contributions and those of his brother, Nicholas (1729–1791), Rhode Island College was renamed Brown University in 1804.

BROWN VS. MARYLAND. In this so-called original-package case, Chief Justice **John Marshall** (*see*) in 1827 expanded on the principle he had established in an earlier case, *Gibbons vs. Ogden* (*see*). According to the commerce clause of the Constitution, the federal government alone had the right to regulate trade between states or other nations. Maryland had passed an act requiring wholesalers of foreign goods to purchase a license from the state. The law was attacked as an unfair tax, and a lawsuit resulted that eventually reached the Supreme Court. Marshall ruled that imported merchandise remaining in the form in which it had arrived could not be taxed by Maryland and was subject only to Congressional regulation. He noted that the Constitution prohibited any state from levying duties on foreign imports, other than those "absolutely necessary for executing [the state's] inspection laws."

BRUNEL, Sir Marc Isambard (1769–1849). Like **Eli Whitney** (*see*), Brunel was among the first to realize the value of interchangeable parts for mass-producing machines and equipment. A native of France, this civil engineer fled the country in 1793 because of his opposition to the French Revolution and came to America. He was appointed a surveyor for a proposed canal between Lake Champlain and the Hudson River. Brunel next became chief engineer of New York City. In 1799, he sailed to England and was able to sell

to the British navy in 1803 his plan for manufacturing pulley blocks with interchangeable parts. Brunel's other inventions included a knitting machine and a machine for manufacturing nails. In 1825, Brunel began work on his greatest project—the first tunnel under the Thames River in England. It was completed in 1843. Brunel was knighted in 1841.

C

CALHOUN, John C. (1782–1850). Born in South Carolina to a wealthy slave-owning family, Calhoun served his country as a Congressman, a Senator, Secretary of War, Vice-President, and Secretary of State. He is best remembered as an impassioned defender of states' rights. As a member (1811–1817) of the House of Representatives, Calhoun was a "war hawk," favoring the United States' entry into the War of 1812. Following the war, he became known as a supporter of a strong Union—a view he was later to change. He backed the establishment of a national bank, highways and canals built at federal expense, and protective tariffs. In

John C. Calhoun

1817, James Monroe (1758–1831) chose Calhoun as his Secretary of War, a post he held until 1825, when he was elected Vice-President under **John Quincy Adams** (*see*). In 1828, Calhoun was again elected Vice-President, this time under **Andrew Jackson** (*see*). His own Presidential ambitions were stymied by the controversy created by the **Tariff of 1828** (*see*). The tariff, called the Tariff of Abominations by the Southern states, resulted in higher prices for imported goods. Calhoun anonymously wrote a letter defending states' rights. In it, he contended that the tariff was unconstitutional and could therefore be nullified by any of the states. (When it later became known that Calhoun had written the letter, his critics labeled him the Great Nullifier.) President Jackson said he would not permit nullification of any federal tariff by South Carolina. As the controversy continued, Calhoun resigned as Vice-President a few months before he was due to leave office and was promptly appointed by the South Carolina legislature to serve in the Senate. Together with **Henry Clay** (*see*), he succeeded in steering a compromise tariff through Congress (*see* **Compromise of 1833**). The slavery issue, which Calhoun feared could destroy the Union, occupied much of the remainder of his career in the Senate (1832–1843 and 1845–1850). He suggested that the United States should have two Presidents, one from the North and one from the South. Each would have veto power, thus preventing one section of the country from dominating the other in Congress. In Senate debates, he defended the system of slavery and insisted that the government could not prohibit slavery in new states. In 1844, as

Secretary of State under President John Tyler (1790–1862), Calhoun argued for the annexation of Texas, which he saw as a potential slave state. His last speech in the Senate was in opposition to the Compromise of 1850, which, among other things, admitted California to the Union as a free state.

A freight-laden barge is pulled by a horse along the towpath of a canal.

CANALS. By providing an efficient and inexpensive method of transportation, canals played an important part in the unification of the nation during the first half of the 19th century. The earliest canals were constructed by private companies and met with little success. By 1816, only three canals were more than two miles long, and most goods were still shipped overland. The same year, **DeWitt Clinton** (*see*) proposed that New York State build a canal connecting Troy, on the Hudson River, with Buffalo, on Lake Erie. The **Erie Canal** (*see*), begun in 1817, was completed in 1825 at a cost of about $7,000,000. It proved to be the first commercially successful canal for the transport of goods from the coast to the interior of the nation (*see pp. 420–421*). It was so profitable that other states were encouraged to construct their own canals. In 1825, Ohio initiated two canal projects—one from Cleveland to Portsmouth, the other from Cincinnati to Toledo—and completed them in 1833. In 1826, Pennsylvania approved a plan for a combined system of canals and railroads stretching from Philadelphia to Pittsburgh (*see p. 421*). The project, which cost more than $10,000,000, was completed in 1834. New Jersey, Maryland, Indiana, Illinois, Michigan, and Wisconsin also completed ambitious canal projects. By the mid-19th century, a network of canals, centered in the North and West, was in operation. New York City, connected to the Erie Canal by the Hudson River, became the nation's largest port. The canals aligned the West commercially with the North and East, rather than the South. Towns and cities developed along the new waterways. However, canal transportation had some disadvantages. Many canals froze during the winter months, and even in summer the boats had to be pulled by horses or mules. With the growth of **railroads** (*see*) in the second half of the 19th century, the importance of canal transportation diminished. Today, only a small percentage of the nation's commerce passes through the system of canals in use in the United States.

CANNING, George (1770–1827). As the British foreign minister in 1823, Canning unintentionally provoked the formulation of the **Monroe Doctrine** (*see*). Due in large part to Canning's eloquence in the House of Commons, Britain had that year recognized the independence of Argentina, Colombia, Chile, Mexico, Brazil, and Central America. In order to prevent possible French and Spanish invasion of these former colonies, Canning appealed to the United States to join Britain in protecting the new republics. As Canning later explained, "I called the New World into existence to redress the balance of the Old." The British leader's call was heard but not heeded by President James Monroe (1758–1831). Concerned also about Russian claims to territory along the Pacific coast, Monroe decided to warn all European nations, including Britain, not to intervene in the Western Hemisphere. This proclamation, issued on December 2, 1823, became known as the Monroe Doctrine.

CHAPPEL, Alonzo (1828–1887). A versatile artist, Chappel painted landscapes, historical events, and pictures of famous personalities such as Andrew Jackson (*see p. 390*). Born in New York City, Chappel was a prodigy who reportedly studied at the National Academy School of Fine Arts in New York at the age of eight and had given two exhibitions of his work by the time he was 17. In his later years, he lived on Long Island and illustrated historical books.

CHEROKEES. One of the most important tribes in the Southeast, the Cherokees farmed and lived in permanent villages. By 1700, they occupied an area stretching from south of the Ohio River to Alabama. From 1721 onward, white

men acquired much of their land by treaties, reducing the Indians' territory to a small area, most of it situated in Georgia. In 1821, a Cherokee named **Sequoyah** (*see*) developed a table of syllables for the Cherokee language, and soon thousands of the Indians were able to read and write. Six years later, the tribe drew up a written constitution establishing the Cherokee Nation in northwestern Georgia. There the Indians built frame houses, roads, and churches and published a weekly newspaper, the *Cherokee Phoenix*. In 1828, Georgia, opposed to an Indian nation within its borders, annexed the land of the Cherokees. The following year, when gold was discovered on Cherokee property, Georgia began to occupy the Indians' land and demanded their removal from the state. A legal battle resulted during which the United States Supreme Court ruled in *Worcester vs. Georgia* (*see*) in 1832 that Georgia had no jurisdiction over the Cherokees' land. With the encouragement of President **Andrew Jackson** (*see*), Georgia ignored the decision. In 1833, a compromise was reached with a small number of Cherokees. A "perpetual outlet, West," known as the Cherokee Strip and located in present-day Oklahoma, was guaranteed to the Indians to encourage their emigration from Georgia. When the rest of the Cherokees refused to move, President **Martin Van Buren** (*see*) ordered in 1838 that they be forced to settle in the Indian Territory in Oklahoma. Under the supervision of American soldiers, they were forced to march 1,000 miles west. About 4,000 of the 13,000 Indians died along the way, and the journey became known as the Trail of Tears (*see p. 396*). In 1892, as the result of government demands, the Indians sold the Cherokee Strip. They disbanded as a tribe and became American citizens in 1906. Almost 4,000 descendants of those Cherokees who escaped the march west or who returned later now live on a reservation in western North Carolina. About 75,000 Cherokee descendants now live in the state of Oklahoma.

CLAY, Henry (1777–1852). Clay's distinguished career in government spanned more than 45 years, many of which he spent trying to hold North and South together. He served as a Senator, a Representative, and Secretary of State and was an unsuccessful candidate for President three times. Clay first entered politics when he was appointed a United States Senator by the Kentucky legislature in 1806. Five years later, as the leader of a group of "war hawks" favoring war with Britain, he was elected to the House of Representatives. On his first day in office, he was chosen Speaker of the House. Shortly after the War of 1812, Clay proposed a series of legislative programs that became known as the American System. The proposals included military reforms, the construction of highways and canals at federal expense, protective tariffs, and a national bank. In foreign affairs, he cooperated with South American revolutionaries in order to improve the leadership position of the United States in the Western Hemisphere. Although a slave owner himself, Clay tried to calm sectional hostilities and was instrumental in guiding the **Missouri Compromise** (*see*) through Congress (1820–1821). For this, he became known as both the Great Pacificator and the Great Compromiser. Clay first ran for President in 1824. Opposing him were **Andrew Jackson,** **John Quincy Adams,** and **William Crawford** (*see all*). No one won a majority of the electoral votes, but Adams won the election when Clay, who had finished last, threw his support to him in the House of Representatives. When President Adams appointed Clay as Secretary of State in 1825, Jackson raised the charge of "Bargain and Sale." Nothing was ever proved, but Clay's opponents used the charge against him when he ran for President against Jackson in 1832 and again in 1844, against James K. Polk (1795–1849). Clay returned to the Senate in 1831, and two years later he was chiefly responsible for working out the tariff settlement known as the **Compromise of 1833** (*see*). He resigned from the Senate in 1842 because President John Tyler (1790–1862), who would not support the American System, consistently vetoed his proposals. It was Clay's wavering on the Texas annexation issue that probably cost him the 1844 Presidential election. He returned to the Senate in 1849, a time of crisis for the nation. The Northern states were insisting that slavery be excluded from the territories acquired as a result of the Mexican War, which had ended the previous year. The Southern states were threatening secession if slavery was excluded. Clay, whose political career was always guided by his admission that he "would rather be right than be President," again sought to prevent open warfare between the North and South. The result of his efforts was the Compromise of 1850, which served to postpone the outbreak of the Civil War for slightly more than a decade.

CLAY COMPROMISE TARIFF. *See* **Compromise of 1833.**

DeWitt Clinton

CLINTON, DeWitt (1769–1828). The man primarily responsible for the construction of the **Erie Canal** (*see*), Clinton began his career in 1790 as private secretary to his uncle, George Clinton (1739–1812), the first governor of New York. DeWitt Clinton himself later became the state's sixth governor. Clinton was elected to the United States Senate in 1802, where he introduced the **Twelfth Amendment** (*see*) to the Constitution. He resigned the following year to become the mayor of New York City, an office he held, except for two annual terms, until 1815. As mayor, Clinton promoted public education as well as social reforms. During part of the time in which he was mayor, he also served as a state senator (1806–1811) and lieutenant governor (1811–1813). Clinton was the unsuccessful Federalist candidate for President in 1812 against James Madison (1751–1836). Appointed to the state canal commission in 1816, Clinton was instrumental in the construction of the Erie Canal (*see p. 420*), which linked the Hudson River with Lake Erie and opened up the West to settlement. During his third term as governor, Clinton took part in the celebrations that opened the canal in 1825.

COHENS VS. VIRGINIA. As a result of this 1821 case, Chief Justice **John Marshall** (*see*) strengthened the doctrine of federal authority over the individual states by ruling that the Supreme Court had the power to review decisions made in state courts. The case arose when two members of the Cohen family were convicted of illegally selling lottery tickets in Virginia. When the Cohens appealed the state's verdict to the Supreme Court, Virginia argued that a federal court had no authority in the case. In his ruling in 1821, Marshall agreed that the Cohens were guilty, but at the same time he denied Virginia's claim that the state courts were exempt from federal review. Thus, the constitutionality of rulings at local levels could be affirmed or denied in appellate courts. Going even further, Marshall interpreted the Eleventh Amendment—which provides that a state cannot be sued by a citizen of another state—to mean that persons, such as the Cohens, were entitled to appeal to a higher authority if the state had initiated the legal action.

COLT, Samuel (1814–1862). Colt invented the first revolver—a pistol with a rotating cylinder. This handgun, which permitted the firing of six bullets without reloading, revolutionized warfare and hunting. Born in Hartford, Connecticut, Colt went to sea when he was 16. He conceived the idea of a repeating firearm while watching the turning of the ship's wheel. Returning to the United States, he secured a patent in 1836 and began the manufacture of his "revolving pistol." At first, Colt's invention met with little acceptance, and his business failed in 1842. Four years later, however, when the Mexican War broke out, the United States Army ordered 1,000 of Colt's .44-caliber pistols, and he reentered business. During the next 20 years, more than 500,000 Colt revolvers were manufactured at his armory in Hartford and sold to the army, Texas Rangers, sheriffs, and cowboys. Both Union and Confederate soldiers employed the weapon during the Civil War.

COMPROMISE OF 1833. By providing for a reduction in tariffs, this compromise, suggested by **Henry Clay** (*see*), prevented a possible civil war with South Carolina. The dispute centered upon the **Ordinance of Nullification** (*see*), by which South Carolina declared null and void the **Tariff of 1828** (*see*) and a subsequent tariff in 1832. President **Andrew Jackson** (*see*) had introduced the **Force Bill** (*see*) in Congress to guarantee the collection of the tariffs. South Carolina then threatened to secede if forced to comply. Clay, fearing that other states would join South Carolina and that a war would break out, introduced a compromise tariff. It provided for a gradual reduction of duties until 1842, when a maximum uniform rate of 20% would be established. The bill was passed by Congress and signed by Jackson on March 2, 1833—the same day that he signed the Force Bill. South Carolina, which had postponed acting upon its Ordinance of Nullification until Congress voted on Clay's compromise, hailed the new tariff law as a victory and rescinded its nullification ordinance on March 15, 1833.

CONESTOGA WAGON. A type of covered wagon, the Conestoga

wagon was the most characteristic means of transportation in America from the mid-18th to the mid-19th century. Historians disagree as to whether its name derives from a breed of horses that had been developed in the Conestoga Valley of Pennsylvania or from the fact that it was originally built there. The wagon was first used between 1750 and 1760 by Pennsylvania farmers to carry their produce to distant markets. It came into widespread use during the half century following the Revolution, when settlers employed it to transport their families and belongings westward across the Allegheny Mountains into the interior of the United States. Eventually, it was used on trips as far west as Utah and the Pacific Northwest. The wooden wagon was invariably painted red and blue and topped by a white cloth cover. It had broad wheels that enabled it to travel long distances over the treacherous dirt roads of the period. The wagon's ends were higher than its middle to prevent its load from shifting and spilling when going up or down hills. The Conestoga, which could carry loads up to eight tons, was drawn by four to six horses. It was the forerunner of the prairie schooner, a canvas-topped wagon that was used in the mid-19th century and required only two to four horses or oxen to pull it.

CONVENTION OF 1818. This treaty between the United States and Britain dealt with specific issues that the Treaty of Ghent (1814), which ended the War of 1812, had left unresolved. The convention provided that the United States be given fishing rights off Labrador and Newfoundland, that a commercial treaty with Britain be renewed,

and that an impartial third nation should settle American claims against the British for slaves captured during the Revolution. The new treaty also fixed the boundary between the United States and Canada. It was to stretch from Lake of the Woods, in present-day Minnesota, to the Rocky Mountains, following the 49th parallel. Under the convention's terms, the Oregon country, a region comprising the Pacific Northwest, was opened to joint occupation by both America and Britain for a period of 10 years, without affecting the territorial rights of either nation. This last stipulation enabled large numbers of Americans to migrate to Oregon. A large portion of that area was later ceded to the United States when the boundary was permanently settled in 1846.

COOPER, Peter (1791–1883). The designer of America's first steam locomotive spent his youth helping his impoverished father in a variety of enterprises, including hat making, brewing, and brick making. At the age of 17, he was apprenticed for $25 a year to a coach maker. In 1821, Cooper

Peter Cooper

purchased a glue factory in New York City, which became the foundation of his fortune. In 1828, he set up an ironworks in Baltimore, Maryland, where he designed and built—for the Baltimore & Ohio Railroad—the first steam locomotive in this country. Named *Tom Thumb,* the engine was pitted against a horse in a seven-mile race near Baltimore on September 18, 1830 (*see pp. 386–387*). Although a mechanical breakdown cost Cooper the race, he proved that trains could be efficiently run, which saved the faltering railroad company. During the next 20 years, Cooper's business interests expanded to include the Trenton ironworks in New Jersey, blast furnaces in Pennsylvania, and foundries in both states. He also helped to finance and promote the laying of the first telegraph cable across the Atlantic Ocean in the 1850s by Cyrus Field (1819–1892). As an inventor, Cooper designed many machines, including a washing machine and an endless chain for moving canalboats. He is remembered best, however, for founding in 1859 the Cooper Union in New York City, which still offers free courses in science and art. At the age of 85, Cooper unsuccessfully ran for President as the Greenback Party candidate, the oldest man ever nominated for the Presidency.

COTTON KINGDOM. The American Deep South between about 1820 and the Civil War is often called the Cotton Kingdom because the cotton industry dominated the economic, social, and political life of the region. Although the climate is ideally suited to the production of cotton, the rise of the Cotton Kingdom would have been impossible

Cotton required slave labor.

without the invention in 1793 of the cotton gin, which mechanically separated the cotton fiber from the seed (*see* **Eli Whitney**). By 1815, cotton was the most valuable American export. However, Northern interests controlled the shipping, trading, and financial backing for the Southern planters. A unique society developed in the South. At the top was a small elite—the proprietors of large plantations, who owned most of the land and the slaves. At the bottom were the slaves, who worked the land and picked the cotton. Most of the white population belonged to a middle group—composed of farmers, businessmen, and professional men—who owned only a small percentage of the kingdom's land and slaves. Because slave labor played such an essential role in the production of cotton, Southern politicians exerted their influence to extend slavery into all newly acquired territory suitable for growing cotton (*see* **Missouri Compromise**). By 1845, the Cotton Kingdom extended from South Carolina to Texas and Arkansas, and its representatives in Congress had a large voice in shaping national policy before the Civil War.

CRAWFORD, William (1772–1834). Born in Virginia to a poverty-stricken family, Crawford settled in Georgia and became a Senator, diplomat, cabinet member, and Presidential candidate. He represented Georgia in the Senate from 1807 until President James Madison (1751–1836) appointed him minister to France in 1813. Upon his return in 1815, Crawford served as Madison's Secretary of War (1815–1816) and then was Secretary of the Treasury (1816–1825) under both Madison and President James Monroe (1758–1831). Crawford was a leading contender for the Presidency until he suffered a stroke in 1823. Although it left him crippled and partly blind, his supporters nevertheless nominated him. In the election of 1824, Crawford finished third to **Andrew Jackson** and **John Quincy Adams** (*see both*) but received more votes in the electoral college than **Henry Clay** (*see*). The election was decided in Adams' favor by the House of Representatives.

CUMBERLAND ROAD. Also called the National Road, the Cumberland Road was the first to be built with federal funds. It was 591 miles long, beginning in Cumberland, Maryland, and running in a northwesterly direction through Pittsburgh to Ohio and on to Vandalia, Illinois. The Cumberland Road partly followed two earlier trails, Nemocolin's Path, also called Cresap's Road, and Braddock's Road. The first was laid out by Nemocolin, a Delaware Indian, for Thomas Cresap, an agent of the Ohio Company. The second was made by the army of General Edward Braddock (1695–1755) on its way to Fort Duquesne in 1755. In 1806, Congress provided for construction of a road from Cumberland to the Ohio River. Begun in 1815, the road stretched as far as Wheeling, in present-day West Virginia, by 1818. The continuation of the highway into Ohio followed the first road built in that state, Zane's Trace, which turned southwestward to Lancaster and the Ohio River. After President James Monroe (1758–1831) vetoed a bill in 1822 providing for federal tollgates on the road, the states assumed control of the highway and it was extended into Indiana and Illinois. Today the Cumberland Road forms part of US Route 40.

D

DANA, Richard Henry (1815–1882). Dana, a student at Harvard, interrupted his studies in 1834 because of poor eyesight and sailed around Cape Horn to California as a seaman on the brig *Pilgrim*. He subsequently described the voyage in *Two Years Before the Mast* (1840), an account of the often brutal life at sea that became a classic in American literature. Public reaction to his vivid description of the treatment of the crew led to reforms in the living conditions of ordinary seamen, who were berthed on sailing ships forward of the mainmast. After graduating from college in 1837, Dana practiced law in Boston. In 1841, he published *The Seaman's Friend,* a manual on seamanship and maritime law for the common sailor. Active in the antislavery movement, Dana served as United States attorney for Massachusetts during the Civil War. From 1867 to 1868, he acted as counsel for the United States in the treason proceedings against Jefferson Davis (1808–1889), the President of the defeated Confederacy. Dana was nominated in 1876 as minister to England by President Ulysses S. Grant (1822–1885), but the Senate refused to confirm him. Dana turned to the study of international law during his last years.

DU PONT, Eleuthere Irenee (1771–1834). Founder of E. I. du Pont de Nemours & Company, du Pont was born in France, where as a young man he worked in the royal powder works at Essonnes. He left there to take charge of his father's publishing house in Paris, which was suppressed by the government in 1797. Du Pont immigrated to America two years later. While hunting with a friend soon after his arrival, du Pont noticed the high price and the poor quality of American gunpowder. Deciding that he could profitably produce a better powder, du Pont returned to France for three months in 1801 to obtain the necessary machinery and designs. He then purchased a farm on the Brandywine River near Wilmington, Delaware, and by 1804 was producing powder. His factory became the principal manufacturer of gunpowder for the government during the War of 1812 and also supplied the American Fur Company and some South American governments. Du Pont explosives were also used to build canals and railroads. Du Pont's company expanded into the production of other chemical products and became one of the largest manufacturers of dyes, lacquers, safety glass, cellophane, nylon, rayon, and plastics.

E

EATON, John Henry (1790–1856). As Secretary of War in the first cabinet of **Andrew Jackson** (*see*), Eaton was involved in a political and social scandal that led to his resignation in 1831, after two years in office. A lawyer, Eaton moved from North Carolina to Tennessee about 1808. There, he married a ward of Jackson's and completed an uncritical biography praising the hero of the Battle of New Orleans (1815). His close relationship with Jackson ensured his political success. Becoming a Senator in 1818, Eaton rented lodgings in a Washington tavern, where he met the owner's married daughter, Peggy Timberlake (*see* **Peggy Eaton**). When Peggy was widowed in 1828, Eaton, whose own wife had died, married her—with the approval of Jackson—to dispel the gossip about their relationship. After Jackson became President two months later on March 4, 1829, he appointed Eaton Secretary of

Peggy Eaton

War. Immediately, Washington society snubbed Peggy. There were rumors that Peggy had already had two children by Eaton and that her first husband had killed himself. Although the President staunchly defended Eaton, he finally accepted his friend's resignation in 1831 and then used the incident to request the resignation of other cabinet officials (*see pp. 393–396*). Eaton served the government in various capacities until 1840, when Jackson's handpicked successor, **Martin Van Buren** (*see*), became President. Personally disliking Van Buren, Eaton ended his friendship with Jackson and retired from political life.

EATON, Peggy O'Neale Timberlake (1796–1879). The bitter opposition of Washington society to Peggy Eaton, the second wife of Secretary of War **John Eaton** (*see*), led to his resignation from the cabinet in 1831. The daughter of a Washington tavern keeper, Peggy was 16 when she married John Timberlake, a purser in the navy. Whenever her husband was at sea, she helped out at her father's inn. There, in 1818, she met Eaton, then a Senator from Tennessee, and soon Washington buzzed with rumors about their relationship. Peggy's husband died at sea in 1828, and Eaton, with the approval of President-elect **Andrew Jackson** (*see*), married her on January 1, 1829. The gossip, however, continued, and when Eaton became Secretary of War two months later, the wives of other cabinet members refused to entertain her. Jackson, a widower who was a friend of Peggy's and whose own wife had been unjustly slandered, rallied to Peggy's support. To vindicate her reputation, Jackson even called a special session of the cabinet, at which he reportedly pronounced Mrs. Eaton "chaste as a virgin." Nevertheless, Peggy remained a social outcast, and her husband was forced to resign his post in 1831. When Eaton served as ambassador to Spain (1836–1840), Peggy was a social success. She became a wealthy widow upon Eaton's death, but she later married an Italian dancing master who ran off with her fortune.

ERIE CANAL. Completed in 1825, this canal provided the first inexpensive and convenient route through the Appalachian Mountains to the West. Under the leadership of Governor **DeWitt Clinton** (*see*), the New York legislature agreed in 1817 to finance the project. Construction began on July 4 of that year. The canal was to run 363 miles from near Troy, on the Hudson River, to Buffalo, on Lake Erie. Plans called for it to be four feet deep and 40 feet wide, with 10-foot-wide towpaths on either side. Eighty-three locks had to be constructed to enable boats to reach the elevation of the lake, which was almost 570 feet above the river level. Immigrants made up the bulk of the labor force. When only 15 miles had been completed during the first two years, critics referred to the canal as Clinton's Ditch and doubted it would ever be completed. However, by 1823, 280 miles were in operation from Albany to Rochester, and the tolls collected from that section were used to pay for the rest of the construction. It was officially completed on October 26, 1825 (*see pp. 432–434*). Because canalboats had neither sails nor oars, all were drawn by horses or mules along the adjacent towpaths. Freight costs from Buffalo to Albany were reduced from $100

to $15 a ton, and the trip took eight days, as opposed to 20 days by land. The canal cost about $7,000,000 to build, but in nine years it had paid for itself, and by 1882, the last year of toll collection, profits had exceeded $42,-000,000. As a result of the canal, the Great Lakes area was opened for settlement, and Buffalo and Rochester grew into important cities. In addition, the canal helped to make New York City the major overseas port in the United States. Seeing the success of the Erie Canal, other states began constructing **canals** (*see*), though none was so financially successful or so significant in the development of the nation.

EVANS, Oliver (1755–1819). This Delaware inventor hastened the arrival of the Industrial Revolution in America by building the nation's first workable steam engine. Learning of the steam experiments performed by James Watt (1736–1819) in England, Evans decided to perfect a steam engine on his own. Meanwhile, he began working at his brothers' flour mill in Wilmington, Delaware, and by 1785 had installed devices that virtually eliminated manual labor in milling operations. After giving up plans to develop a steam-powered carriage for lack of funds, Evans concentrated on designing a stationary, high-pressure steam engine. He successfully completed it by 1802 and soon afterward received financial backing for further experiments. In 1803, Evans began constructing engines on a regular basis and the next year built a steam-operated river dredge. Nicknamed Orukter Amphibolos (*see p. 382*), the machine sailed on its own power from Evans' mill in Delaware to the Schuylkill River at

Philadelphia. By the time of his death in 1819, 50 of his steam engines were being used in various industries along the Atlantic coast.

EWING, Thomas (1789–1871). Ewing served the nation as a Senator, Secretary of the Treasury, and the first Secretary of the Interior. Born in Virginia, Ewing moved as a young boy to Ohio and later became a lawyer. He was first elected to the Senate in 1830 and denounced President **Andrew Jackson** (*see*) for removing federal deposits from the **Second Bank of the United States** (*see*) in 1833. President **William Henry Harrison** (*see*) appointed Ewing Secretary of the Treasury in 1841, and as such he fought for the reestablishment of a national bank. When, after Harrison's death, President John Tyler (1790–1862) vetoed two bank bills, Ewing resigned and went back to Ohio to practice law. In 1849, President Zachary Taylor (1784–1850) appointed Ewing to the newly created cabinet post of Secretary of the Interior. When Taylor died, Ewing resigned his position and returned to the Senate. He retired in 1851 but later served President Abraham Lincoln (1809–1865) as an adviser.

F

FORCE BILL. Signed on March 2, 1833, the Force Bill authorized President **Andrew Jackson** (*see*) to use the army and the navy to enforce tariff laws. South Carolina had threatened to secede if required to collect the **Tariff of 1828** (*see*). The bill was only a token gesture of federal authority, because the tariff had been repealed by the **Compromise of 1833** (*see*). It was, however, the first time a

President had threatened the use of military force to prevent a state from seceding.

FORSYTH, John (1780–1841). Forsyth, an able statesman and orator, was one of the staunchest supporters of the policies of **Andrew Jackson** (*see*). Born in Fredericksburg, Virginia, Forsyth became a lawyer in 1802 and began his political career six years later as attorney general of Georgia. He subsequently served in Washington as a Representative (1813–1818) and as a Senator (1818). As minister (1819–1823) to Spain, Forsyth obtained the Spanish king's ratification of the **Adams-Onis Treaty** (*see*), by which Spain ceded the Floridas to the United States. He again served as a Representative (1823–1827) and then was governor of Georgia (1827–1829) before returning to the Senate (1829–1834). Forsyth backed Jackson in his fight against nullification (*see* **Ordinance of Nullification**), supported the **Force Bill** (*see*) of 1833, and justified Jackson's stand against rechartering the **Second Bank of the United States** (*see*). In 1834, Jackson rewarded Forsyth by making him Secretary of State, a position he held until the year of his death.

G

GAG RULE. A gag rule was a rule of the House of Representatives that enabled a majority of the Representatives to suppress or limit debate. The most noted of such restrictions was adopted by proslavery Congressmen at each annual session of Congress between 1836 and 1844. This rule automatically "shelved" petitions concerning slavery that were received by the House. The first such rule was introduced in May, 1836, by Southern legislators in an attempt to suppress the growing wave of antislavery sentiment in the country. For the next eight years, former President **John Quincy Adams** (*see*) was the most eloquent opponent of these rules. Adams was not an abolitionist, but he objected to the gag rule on the ground that it violated the right to petition guaranteed by the First Amendment to the Constitution. In December, 1844, the use of gag rules was abandoned.

GIBBONS VS. OGDEN. In his decision on this so-called steamboat case in 1824, Chief Justice **John Marshall** (*see*) increased the authority of the federal government over the states by broadly interpreting the part of the Constitution known as the commerce clause. The clause gives Congress the power "to regulate" commerce between the states and with foreign nations. The state of New York had granted Aaron Ogden (1756–1839) exclusive rights to operate a passenger steamboat line between New York City and Elizabethtown, New Jersey. When Thomas Gibbons (1757–1826), who had a federal license, ran two steamboats in competition with Ogden's, Ogden sued and the case was appealed to the Supreme Court. Marshall ruled in favor of Gibbons. He defined commerce to include not only buying or selling but also transportation and routes. Although Marshall agreed that a state could regulate trade within its boundaries, he said trade carried across state lines was subject to national authority. As a result of his ruling, competition among steamboat owners was encouraged and led to low fares and good service. Marshall's decision also set a precedent for later federal control over interstate power lines and television and radio broadcasts.

GOODYEAR, Charles (1800–1860). Goodyear, who was born in New Haven, Connecticut, invented the process of vulcanizing rubber. In 1834, when he first started experimenting with rubber, the main problem facing its manufacturers was that it decomposed, melted, and became sticky in the heat. After 10 years of experimentation, Goodyear finally perfected vulcanization, which prevented these effects. The process, which is accomplished by mixing rubber with sulfur and then heating it, was patented in the United States in 1844 and then in Europe after 1851. Goodyear's experiments were so costly that he was unable to profit commercially from his discovery. He was forced to sell licenses for his process so cheaply that he lived most of his life in poverty and died in debt. The Goodyear Tire & Rubber Company was named after him, although it has no connection with him or his family.

Charles Goodyear

GRUNDY, Felix (1777–1840). Grundy took the Senate seat of **John Eaton** (*see*) of Tennessee when Eaton was appointed Secretary of War by President **Andrew Jackson** (*see*) in 1829. After Eaton resigned his cabinet post in 1831, he tried to regain his place in the Senate, and the result was a bitter struggle in the Tennessee legislature. Despite Jackson's support of Eaton, the legislators sent Grundy back to the Senate in 1833. A native of Virginia, Grundy was raised in Kentucky. He became a lawyer in 1797, and in 1806 he was appointed to the state supreme court, where he soon became chief justice. He resigned his position the following year because it paid so little and moved to Tennessee, where he became a noted criminal lawyer and a political ally of Jackson. Grundy was twice elected to the House of Representatives (1811–1815) before serving in the Senate (1829–1838). He was appointed Attorney General in 1838 by President **Martin Van Buren** (*see*) but quit that post the following year to reenter the Senate. He died in office in 1840.

H

HARRISON, William Henry (1773–1841). Harrison, ninth President of the United States and hero of the Battle of Tippecanoe, died one month after he was inaugurated. Born in Virginia, Harrison gave up the study of medicine to enter the army in 1791. He took part in campaigns against the Indians in the Old Northwest, which included the land north of the Ohio River. Seven years later, he was appointed secretary of the Northwest Territory, and in 1799 he was elected its first delegate to

Congress. For the next 12 years, Harrison served as governor of the Indiana Territory, obtaining millions of acres of land for the United States through treaties with the Indians. Resentful of the increasing encroachment by settlers, the Indians banded together under the Shawnee chieftain Tecumseh (1768–1813). Their opposition was broken when Harrison defeated Tecumseh's warriors near an Indian village on Tippecanoe Creek on November 7, 1811. During the War of 1812, Harrison, now a brigadier general, was put in command of the Army of the Northwest. He recaptured Detroit from the British in September, 1813. The following month, Harrison's troops decisively defeated the British and killed Tecumseh in the Battle of the Thames in Ontario, Canada, thus ending the threat of any future British invasion and further Indian raids in the Northwest. Before the war ended, Harrison retired to his farm in North Bend, Ohio, but left in 1816 to serve three years as a member of the House of Representatives. In 1819, he was elected to the Ohio senate and six years later to the United States Senate. After three years in the Senate, Harrison was appointed minister to Colombia but was recalled the following year when his sympathies for native revolutionaries annoyed Colombian officials. He was nominated by the Whigs to run against **Martin Van Buren** (*see*) in the Presidential election of 1836. Although he lost, Harrison received so many popular votes that the Whigs nominated him to run again against Van Buren in the next election. John Tyler (1790–1862) of Virginia was his running mate. The campaign of 1840 was a flamboyant one, during which the slogan "Tippe-

canoe and Tyler too" was often heard. Harrison, called the "log cabin and hard cider" candidate, was elected. On his chilly Inauguration Day, he declined to wear either a hat or a coat, and exhausted from the campaign, caught cold. He died of pneumonia on April 4, 1841, the first President to die in office.

HART, Joel Tanner (1810–1877). A native of Kentucky, Hart achieved fame by sculpturing many prominent personalities of his time. Using scientific methods, including photographs and facial casts, he produced realistic likenesses of national figures. Among those he portrayed in stone were President **Andrew Jackson** and **Henry Clay** (*see both*). His bust of Clay is now in the Corcoran Art Gallery in Washington, D.C. Having established his artistic reputation in the United States, Hart moved his studio to Florence, Italy, in 1849. Nine years later, he patented a machine that measured the features of his subjects. He died in Florence on March 2, 1877.

HAWTHORNE, Nathaniel (1804–1864). One of America's greatest novelists and short-story writers, Hawthorne was born in Salem, Massachusetts, the son of a sea captain. After graduation from Bowdoin College in 1825, Hawthorne remained in Salem for 12 years, reading, writing, and traveling throughout New England in the summers. It was a period of isolation and self-analysis, during which Hawthorne wrote the stories published in 1837 under the title *Twice-Told Tales*. From 1839 to 1841, he worked in the Boston customhouse, using his free time to write children's stories. In 1842, after spending

Nathaniel Hawthorne

less than a year participating in an experiment in communal living, Hawthorne moved to nearby Concord, the home of Ralph Waldo Emerson (1803–1882) and Henry David Thoreau (1817–1862). There he wrote *Mosses from an Old Manse,* a collection of stories. In need of money, he returned to Salem and worked as surveyor of the port from 1846 to 1849. The next year, he published his first successful novel, *The Scarlet Letter.* This book, which examined the Puritan conscience in the era of the notorious Salem witchcraft trials of 1692, was followed in 1851 by *The House of the Seven Gables* and *The Snow-Image.* In 1852, he published *The Blithedale Romance* and a children's book. The following year, Hawthorne was appointed the United States consul at Liverpool, England, by his college friend, President Franklin Pierce (1804–1869). For the next seven years, Hawthorne lived and worked in Europe. He published only one more novel and a collection of essays before his death. Hawthorne is buried in Sleepy Hollow Cemetery, Concord.

HAYNE, Robert Young (1791–1839). As Senator from South Carolina, Hayne engaged in a famous debate with Daniel Webster (1782–1852) that summed up the basic differences between the North and the South (*see* **Webster-Hayne Debate**). During his time in the Senate (1823–1832), Hayne consistently opposed the Democrats' policy of protective tariffs. He believed that they were unconstitutional, that they favored Eastern manufacturers, and that they pitted one section of the nation against another. In 1830, Hayne and Webster debated for nearly two weeks over issues that ranged from tariffs and slavery to the rights of the states versus the federal government. Hayne resigned from the Senate in 1832 and was elected governor of South Carolina (1832–1834). He led his state in nullifying the Tariff of 1832 (*see* **Ordinance of Nullification**) and even called 10,000 men to arms to repel an expected attack by the federal government. This became unnecessary when Congress lowered the tariff by the **Compromise of 1833** (*see*).

HONE, Philip (1780–1851). A socialite and one-time mayor of New York, Hone wrote a diary (1828–1851) that is a valuable chronicle of life in that city. In 1796, Hone became an auctioneer and within five years was a partner in one of the most prosperous auction firms in the city. He had accumulated a fortune estimated at more than $500,000 by 1821, when he retired from business to devote himself to civic affairs. Elected mayor in 1825, he endeavored to further the city's culture, often entertaining the leading personalities in the arts, business, and politics. Hone invested in the Delaware-Hudson Canal and in coal mines in Pennsylvania, where a town, Honesdale, was named in his honor. After the Whig Party was founded in 1836, Hone became a close associate of **Henry Clay** (*see*) and Daniel Webster (1782–1852). He ran on the Whig ticket for the state senate in 1839, but lost.

Philip Hone

HOWE, Elias (1819–1867). The inventor of the sewing machine first developed his mechanical skill while repairing and tinkering with the machinery in his father's Massachusetts gristmill and sawmill. At the age of 16, young Howe moved to nearby Lowell to work in a factory that made cotton looms. Two years later, in 1837, he apprenticed himself to a Cambridge watchmaker, who also made scientific instruments for Harvard College. While in Cambridge, Howe began to design a machine that would sew with a motion similar to that of the human hand. By 1845, he had completed a model that sewed at

METROPOLITAN MUSEUM OF ART: GIFT OF I. N. PHELPS STOKES, EDWARD S. HAWES, ALICE MARY HAWES, MARION AUGUSTA HAWES, 1937

Elias Howe

a speed of 250 stitches a minute, five times faster than the swiftest seamstress. He was issued a patent the next year, but finding no market for his invention, sent his brother to England with a model of the machine. Howe's brother sold the model, together with all British rights, to William Thomas, an English corset manufacturer. Thomas saw greater possibilities for the invention and invited Elias Howe to come work in England at a salary of $15 a week. Within a year, the two men had quarreled and ended their association. Howe raised enough money by pawning his patent papers to return to America, where he discovered that several manufacturers had begun to make and sell sewing machines that were similar to his. Howe sued and won. In 1854, the courts declared Howe's invention to be the basic one in the field. **Isaac Singer** (*see*), the most successful manufacturer, was forced to pay $25 in royalties on every machine he sold. These royalties often amounted to thousands of dollars a week. During the Civil War, Howe formed and outfitted a Connecticut infantry regiment in which he served as a private. In 1865, he founded the Howe Machine Company and perfected a sewing machine that was awarded a gold medal in the Paris Exhibition of 1867.

IMMIGRATION. Following the War of 1812, a constant stream of immigrants began to arrive in America (*see pp. 458–459 and 851*). So many came between 1820 and 1880 that the period became known as the Old Migration. The majority came from nations in northern and western Europe, Ireland, Germany, England, and Scandinavia. The Irish, fleeing poverty and the famine of 1846, provided much of the labor force for new industries and the building of canals and railroads. The Germans, uprooted by economic distress like the Irish, settled in New York, Baltimore, Cincinnati, and St. Louis, where they became craftsmen. Those who emigrated after the Revolution of 1848 in Germany were highly educated in law, medicine, and teaching. Milwaukee virtually became a German city. The Scandinavians generally settled on farms in Nebraska, Minnesota, and Wisconsin. Chinese immigrants contributed greatly to the labor force, building the railroads in the West. After the Panic of 1857 and the outbreak of the Civil War four years later, immigration declined. It was not a major factor in the nation's growth again until the 1870s. The "New Immigration"— from Slavic nations and Italy —began the following decade.

INDUSTRIAL REVOLUTION. During the 77 years between the Revolution and the Civil War, American industry gradually assumed a major role in the nation's economy. A number of factors aided this industrial growth— including the invention of certain machinery (notably the cotton gin and cotton-spinning machines),

immigration (*see*), and improved transportation (*see* **canals, steamboats,** and **railroads**). As the nation grew, there was an increasing demand for farm and factory equipment to satisfy the need for more crops, clothing, and other goods. In the New England states, where fast-flowing rivers provided waterpower, a textile industry began with the construction of a spinning frame and two carding machines (*see pp. 380–381*) by **Samuel Slater** (*see*) in 1790. Two years later, **Eli Whitney** (*see*) invented the cotton gin. Whitney was also responsible for inventing interchangeable parts, a system that made mass production possible (*see pp. 378–379*). Sawmills with rotary saws were built in Minnesota and Michigan. Wheat production soared after **Cyrus McCormick** (*see*) began manufacturing his celebrated reaper in 1837, and flour milling soon became the nation's largest industry in the early 19th century. An iron industry developed in Pennsylvania, New York, New Jersey, and Kentucky—areas where ore and fuel were available—and the wrought iron it produced was used extensively in machinery and tools.

IRVING, Washington (1783–1859). The author of "Rip Van Winkle" and "The Legend of Sleepy Hollow" was born in New York City, the youngest of 11 children of a successful businessman. As a boy, he showed little interest in schoolwork, but he read widely. Later, he practiced law for a while before writing humorous newspaper articles under the pseudonym of Jonathan Oldstyle, Gent. Between 1807 and 1809, Irving devoted himself to satirical writings, climaxed by the publication of *A History of New York from the Beginning of the World to the End of* the Dutch Dynasty (1809). Written under another fictitious name, Diedrich Knickerbocker, this book is regarded as the first piece of American comic literature. Irving served briefly as a colonel in the War of 1812, after which he made his home in Europe until 1832. There he met Sir Walter Scott (1771–1832), who encouraged his writing. In 1820, Irving published his famous *Sketch Book of Geoffrey Crayon, Gent.*, which brought him immediate acclaim as America's foremost author. These classic sketches, including the well-known stories about Rip Van Winkle and Sleepy Hollow, dealt with scenes and folk legends of the Hudson River Valley. Other less successful books followed, including *Bracebridge Hall* (1822), *Tales of a Traveller* (1824), a biography of Christopher Columbus (1828), a volume on the American frontier (1835), and a history (1836) of the family of John Jacob Astor (1763–1848). After serving as minister to Spain (1842–1846), Irving settled at his estate in Tarrytown, New York, to work on various books, including a five-volume biography (1855–1859) of George Washington. Although not as brilliant a writer as his contemporary, **Nathaniel Hawthorne** (*see*), Irving was an important influence on early American literature and its cultural heritage.

J

JACKSON, Andrew (*Continued from Volume 4*). Jackson, the hero of the Battle of New Orleans (1815), continued to receive national publicity as a soldier following the War of 1812. His rash attack on the **Seminoles** (*see*) in Spanish-controlled East Florida in 1818 provoked a public furor

(*see also* **Arbuthnot-Ambrister Affair**). The Spanish officials wanted Jackson punished for invading their territory, but Secretary of State **John Quincy Adams** (*see*) refused. After the United States bought the Floridas from Spain in 1819, Jackson was appointed the new territory's first governor in 1821. He next served as United States Senator (1823–1825) from Tennessee. Jackson ran for President in 1824. He won the most popular votes and received the most electoral votes, but neither he nor his rivals—**William Crawford, Henry Clay** (*see both*), and Adams—won a majority. Adams, with Clay's support, was subsequently elected President by the House of Representatives. Determined to win the next election in 1828, Jackson's supporters promoted their candidate as the champion of democracy and the common man. Their efforts were successful, and in 1829 he became the seventh President. However, the campaign had been an especially bitter one, and when his wife, Rachel, died before his inauguration, Jackson blamed her death on the abuse she had received. Once in office, Jackson rewarded many of his supporters with governmental positions. He thus was credited with originating the **spoils system** (*see*), as this practice became known after 1831, although in fact it had been going on since George Washington's first term in office. What Jackson did was to employ it to a greater extent than any previous President. Jackson's first administration (1829–1833) was marred by his personal and political feud with his Vice-President, **John C. Calhoun** (*see*). A major disagreement involved Jackson's close friend and Secretary of War, **John Eaton** (*see*). His wife, **Peggy Eaton**

Andrew Jackson

(*see*), was snubbed by Mrs. Floride Calhoun and the other cabinet wives because of widespread rumors of improper conduct. This enraged Jackson. Not long afterward, President Jackson clashed with Calhoun over the question of states' rights. Calhoun, a native of South Carolina, considered the **Tariff of 1828** (*see*), known in the South as the Tariff of Abominations, too high. Calhoun advocated nullification, which meant that any state could nullify a federal law—in this case, a tariff law. Jackson, who realized that this could lead to civil war, held that federal authority was supreme. Their argument erupted at a famous dinner on April 13, 1830. To Jackson's toast, "Our Federal Union, it must be preserved!" Calhoun replied, "The Union, next to our liberty, most dear." Calhoun finally resigned from the Vice-Presidency in 1832 to advance the cause of nullification in the Senate. Only after Jackson threatened in March, 1833, to use federal troops to uphold federal authority (*see* **Force Bill**) was a compromise tariff finally arranged (*see* **Compromise of 1833**). In the meantime, Jackson had been re-elected in November, 1832, by an overwhelming majority. The main issue of that campaign was the re-chartering of the **Second Bank of the United States** (*see*). Jackson had made known his opposition to the bank the previous July, when he vetoed a bill calling for its rechartering. Jackson, who dis-liked banks in general, opposed the federal institution on the ground that it was unconstitutional and had developed a private monopoly of federal funds. Once reelected, he withdrew all federal funds from the bank, placing them in state banks, which became known as pet banks. His **Specie Circular** (*see*) of July, 1836, stated that the government would accept only gold and silver in payment for land. This ruling was partly responsible for the financial **Panic of 1837** (*see*). On the diplomatic scene, Jackson's accomplishments were significant. He established trade with the British West Indies for the first time since the American Revolution and also secured a payment from France for American claims dating from the Napoleonic Wars. After his hand-picked successor, **Martin Van Buren** (*see*), was inaugurated in 1837, Jackson returned to The Hermitage, his estate near Nash-ville. The old frontiersman was 78 when he died at his home on June 8, 1845.

JOHNSON, Richard M. (1780–1850). The ninth Vice-President of the United States, Johnson began his political career as a member of the legislature in Kentucky, where he was a successful lawyer.

In 1807, he was elected to the first of 10 terms in the House of Representatives. During the War of 1812, he recruited a regiment of mounted riflemen, which he commanded in victories over the British and Indians in Canada. Johnson was a member (1819–1829) of the Senate before returning to the House, where he served until 1836. That year, he was one of the candidates for the Vice-Presidency. He was elected by the Senate when no candidate received a majority in the electoral college—the only Vice-President ever so chosen (*see* **Twelfth Amendment**). Johnson ran for reelection in 1840, but he was defeated and retired from public life.

K

KENDALL, Amos (1789–1869). Born in Massachusetts and trained as a lawyer, Kendall moved to Kentucky in 1814 and became a journalist. As editor of the influential *Argus of Western America,* he helped **Andrew Jackson** (*see*) carry that state in the Presidential election of 1828. For the next eight years, Kendall was one of the most trusted members of Jackson's "kitchen cabinet," an informal group of Presidential advisers. For six of those years, Kendall's official position was fourth auditor of the Treasury. In 1835, he was appointed Postmaster General by Jackson. Kendall eliminated much of the corruption in the Post Office and cleared up the department's debt. He retired in 1840 because of ill health. Kendall tried to become a publisher but by 1845 had fallen into debt. He then became the legal and business agent for **Samuel F. B. Morse** (*see*) and worked vigorously to protect the patent rights for Morse's newly invented telegraph. During the next 14 years, both men made fortunes. Before his death, Kendall contributed generously to various religious and charitable organizations.

KRIMMEL, John Lewis (1789–1821). Krimmel was one of the few artists of his time to capture on canvas the everyday happenings of American life. Soon after arriving in Philadelphia from Germany in 1810, Krimmel decided to earn his living painting. His keen eyesight and qualities of observation made him a popular portrait artist, although his real interest lay in such typically American subjects as a Fourth of July celebration or an election-day scene (*see p. 364*).

L

LANCASTER TURNPIKE. This 62-mile toll road from Philadelphia to Lancaster, Pennsylvania, begun in 1791 and completed in 1797, was the first turnpike built in the United States. It was a privately financed road constructed

Amos Kendall

by the Philadelphia and Lancaster Turnpike Company, which sold 1,000 shares of stock at $300 a share to build it. The opening of the road encouraged settlement in the interior of the nation, and large numbers of pioneers traveled west in **Conestoga wagons** (*see*) over the Lancaster Pike. In 1798, traffic increased with the establishment of a 12-hour night stage service between Philadelphia and Lancaster. The financial success of the road encouraged the construction of other toll roads, among them the Knoxville Road, the Wilderness Road, and the Old Walton Road. The Lancaster Turnpike lost much of its traffic when the main line of the Pennsylvania Railroad was built parallel to it in the mid-1850s. Toll charges were finally dropped in 1917, when the state purchased the road.

LATROBE, Benjamin (1764–1820). Latrobe, an English-born civil engineer, was America's leading architect in the early years of the new nation. In 1796, he emigrated to Virginia, where he helped to improve navigation on the Appomattox and James Rivers. The following year, he designed the Richmond Penitentiary, the first prison built with single cells for inmates. In 1799, Latrobe won a competition to design the Bank of Pennsylvania at Philadelphia. His concept—the building was meant to look like a Greek temple—became known as the Greek revival style and thereafter dominated American architecture for nearly 60 years. Latrobe engineered Philadelphia's first waterworks, which carried water to a reservoir from the nearby Schuylkill River by means of steam-operated pumps. Two years after its completion in 1801, President Thomas Jefferson (1743–1826)

named Latrobe the surveyor of public buildings in Washington, D.C. For the next 14 years, Latrobe worked on many of the federal offices. After the British burned the Capitol and White House during the War of 1812, he remodeled and rebuilt both buildings. Besides working on numerous government and private commissions, Latrobe also surveyed lands from New York to New Orleans and recorded his observations in sketches and watercolors (*see p. 425*). He died of yellow fever while engaged in building a waterworks in New Orleans.

LEWIS, William B. (1784–1866). A longtime friend in Nashville of President **Andrew Jackson** (*see*), Lewis served efficiently as Jackson's quartermaster during the War of 1812. He later helped to publicize Jackson's first Presidential campaign. When Jackson took office in 1829, Lewis went to live with the President at the White House. He became a member of

Jackson's unofficial "kitchen cabinet" while holding the official position of second auditor of the Treasury. His most notable political contribution was an attempt to conciliate the opposing factions in the Eaton controversy (*see* **Peggy Eaton**). He remained in his post when **Martin Van Buren** (*see*) became President in 1837.

M

McCORMICK, Cyrus (1809–1884). McCormick revolutionized farming methods in the United States and throughout the world by inventing and manufacturing a mechanical harvester. His father, Robert McCormick (1780–1846), had invented and patented farming implements in Virginia, but in 20 years of experimenting he had never come up with a workable reaper. In 1831, Cyrus successfully tested a reaper of his own design, based on the principle of a moving knife against a fixed metal

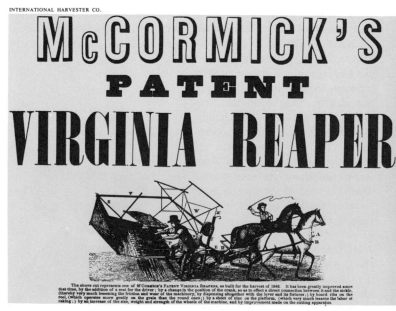

An 1848 print shows the reaper that revolutionized world farming methods.

finger, and shortly produced an improved model that contained features still found in modern reapers (*see pp. 384–385*). He patented the machine in 1834, a year after Obed Hussey (1792–1860) of Cincinnati patented a similar device. McCormick began manufacturing his reaper in 1837. Ten years later, he started large-scale operations at a factory in Chicago which eventually became the International Harvester Company. Europeans first saw the reaper in 1851 at the Great Exposition in London. By 1860, McCormick had 100 competitors, but he managed to survive them all, and he and his engineers continued perfecting the machine. McCormick's invention had far-reaching consequences. Farmers could now produce a greater yield with less cost and labor. Workers, no longer needed on the farm, migrated to the cities and entered industry. During the Civil War, there was even a surplus of wheat, which was exported to Europe and helped the federal government pay the cost of the war.

McCULLOCH VS. MARYLAND.

In this landmark case of American law, the Supreme Court unanimously upheld in 1819 the constitutionality of the **Second Bank of the United States** (*see*). In so doing, the Court gave judicial approval to what it called the "implied powers" of Congress. When the federal bank, chartered by Congress in 1816, began forming state branches, the local private banks resented the competition. In Maryland, as in other states, the legislature voted an annual tax on the national bank, which refused to pay it. Maryland then sued the national bank's cashier, James W. McCulloch. In ruling on the case, Chief Justice

John Marshall (*see*) first explained that although the Constitution did not specifically empower Congress to create a national bank, the authority to do so was implied because the bank helped Congress perform such functions as coining money and regulating currency. Thus, because the bank was legal, Maryland had performed an unconstitutional act by taxing a government agency.

McLANE, Louis (1786–1857).

This American statesman and diplomat entered the navy as a midshipman at the age of 12 and served for three years. Afterward, he became a lawyer in Delaware and was elected in 1817 to the House of Representatives, where he served for the next 10 years. In 1827, McLane became a Senator but resigned two years later when he was appointed minister to Britain. Recalled in 1831 to serve as Secretary of the Treasury, he differed with President **Andrew Jackson** (*see*) over the rechartering of the **Second Bank of the United States** (*see*) and was shifted to Secretary of State in 1833, a post he held for one year. After resigning from the cabinet, McLane became president of the Morris Canal & Banking Company in New York in 1834, and three years later he took over control of the Baltimore & Ohio Railroad. In 1845, President James K. Polk (1795–1849) appointed McLane minister to England, where he helped to negotiate the Oregon boundary compromise in 1846.

MANN, Horace (1796–1859).

Mann is often called the father of American public education. Born in Massachusetts, he had an unhappy childhood. His family was poor, and what education he received was from ignorant and

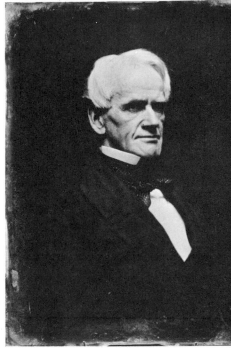

Horace Mann

cruel teachers. Although he never attended school for more than 10 weeks in any year of his youth, Mann graduated from Brown University with high honors in 1819. He became a lawyer four years later and then served (1827–1837) in the state legislature, where he was instrumental in establishing the Massachusetts board of education. As secretary (1837–1848) of this board, he aroused public interest in free education, instituted better training for teachers, raised their salaries, and improved teaching methods and equipment. He also sponsored a law in 1839 setting the annual school term at a minimum of six months, and he helped to establish more than 50 new high schools. The 12 annual reports that he prepared as secretary of the board were invaluable documents. In them, he analyzed the problems and needs of public education and made suggestions as to how these problems could be corrected. Mann served (1848–1853) in the House of Representatives and in 1852 was an unsuccessful candidate for the governorship of Massachusetts. As president (1853–1859) of Antioch College in Ohio, Mann summarized his philosophy when he told the graduating class of 1859, "Be ashamed to die until you have won some victory for humanity."

MARBURY VS. MADISON. In this 1803 case, the Supreme Court, presided over by **John Marshall** (*see*), applied the principle of judicial review of Congress for the first time by declaring a federal law unconstitutional. President John Adams (1735–1826), in the last days of his administration, signed a commission appointing William Marbury to be a justice of the peace in the District of Columbia. Adams' successor, Thomas Jefferson (1743–1826), prohibited his Secretary of State, James Madison (1751–1836), from delivering the commission. Marbury then petitioned the Supreme Court for a writ of mandamus to force Madison to give him his commission. A writ of mandamus is an order directing a government official to perform a specific act. Although aware that Marbury was entitled to his commission, Chief Justice Marshall ruled that the Supreme Court did not have the power to issue this writ. Such power had been conferred upon the Court in Section 13 of the Judiciary Act, which was passed by Congress in 1789. But Marshall argued that this act was unconstitutional because it had in effect changed the original powers granted the Court by the Constitution. By nullifying Section 13 of the Judiciary Act, the Court thus asserted its authority to be the final interpreter of the Constitution. The ruling also set a precedent for lower courts to follow at the state level, and it helped to make the American court system the strongest in the world.

MARSHALL, John (1755–1835). As the third Chief Justice of the United States, Marshall raised the Supreme Court to a position of power equal to that of the President and of Congress. Born on the Virginia frontier, Marshall had little formal schooling, although he briefly attended a law course at the College of William and Mary. He was admitted to the Virginia bar in 1780 and three years later settled in Richmond. He soon acquired a reputation as a brilliant courtroom debater, with a gift for reducing arguments to essentials. In 1787, Marshall was instrumental in getting Virginia to ratify the United States Constitution. He advocated a strong system of federal courts, saying, "To what quarter will you look for protection from an infringement of the Constitution, if you will not give the power to the judiciary?" He subsequently became a Federalist and was elected to the House of

JOHN MARSHALL, *Chief Justice of the U.S. 1801.*

Representatives in 1799. The following year he was appointed Secretary of State by President John Adams (1735–1826). Before Adams left office in 1801, he named Marshall Chief Justice of the Supreme Court. Until then, the Court had decided no issues of importance. With Marshall presiding, however, it quickly emerged as a major power in government. The decisions that Marshall wrote during the next 34 years formed an important body of constitutional doctrine. His opinions were based on a loose interpretation of the Constitution and took into account the document's implied as well as its specifically listed powers. These decisions served to strengthen national unity in the early years of the Republic. In the very first one of importance, *Marbury vs. Madison* (*see*) in 1803, Marshall said the Supreme Court had the authority to declare state and federal laws unconstitutional and void, and thereby established the principle of judicial review. Gradually thereafter, Marshall, who had always distrusted narrow state interests, gave precedence to the federal government over the states. In a series of decisions—*McCulloch vs. Maryland, Cohens vs. Virginia, Gibbons vs. Ogden, Brown vs. Maryland,* and *Worcester vs. Georgia* (*see all*)—Marshall ruled in favor of the federal government, thus curtailing the jurisdiction of the states. In all, he wrote nearly half of the more than 1,100 opinions handed down by the Supreme Court during his term in office.

MARTINEAU, Harriet (1802–1876). Miss Martineau was an English writer and social reformer who toured the United States (1834–1836). She subsequently published *Society in America*

Harriet Martineau

(1837) and *Retrospect of Western Travel* (1838). The first book—which was a basically sympathetic analysis of American social, economic, and political practices—was extremely critical of slavery and provoked considerable controversy. The second, which was written in a lighter vein, recounted her travel experiences. Before and during the Civil War, Miss Martineau also contributed numerous articles to English and American newspapers in defense of the abolition movement.

MISSOURI COMPROMISE.

The Missouri Compromise, which was actually two compromises, temporarily resolved the growing national dispute over slavery. In 1817, the Missouri Territory first petitioned Congress for statehood. In 1819, Representative **James Tallmadge** (*see*) of New York shocked the South by offering an amendment prohibiting the introduction of slaves into Missouri and freeing all slaves born in Missouri after its admission, once they reached the age of 25. His amendment was passed in February by the House, where the Northern members were in the

majority. However, it was defeated 11 to 10 in the Senate, even though the slave states were outnumbered. A number of Northern Senators, born and brought up in the South, voted with the slave states. Congress then adjourned without settling the Missouri question. When it reconvened in December, 1819, Alabama was admitted to the Union as a slave state. When Maine petitioned Congress for statehood, **Henry Clay** (*see*) supported a suggestion that it be admitted as a free state, thus balancing Missouri as a slave state. Senator **Jesse Thomas** (*see*) of Illinois introduced a compromise amendment that admitted Missouri as a slave state. But it also provided that any other new states from the Louisiana Territory north of 36° 30′ latitude (the southern boundary of Missouri) would be free states. A bitter debate followed, but in March, 1820, both sides agreed to the compromise. The North won a ban on slavery in a vast Western territory, and Maine was admitted as a free state on March 15, 1820. The

South, in turn, had won the admission of Missouri as a slave state. This became known as the Missouri Compromise. However, trouble arose when Congress had to approve Missouri's constitution, which excluded blacks from the state. A second compromise, formulated largely by Clay, was arranged. Under it, Missouri's state legislature agreed never to deny the privileges and immunities guaranteed to all citizens of the United States, and on August 10, 1821, Missouri became a state.

MONROE DOCTRINE.

In his annual message to Congress on December 2, 1823, President James Monroe (1758–1831) made several remarks concerning American foreign policy that ultimately became known as the Monroe Doctrine and still remain the basis for United States policy toward Latin America. Monroe, although urged by the British to issue a joint warning against European intervention in the Americas, decided instead to assert America's sole

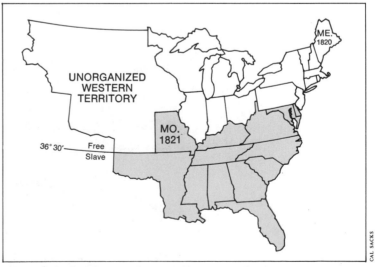

Shaded area shows where slavery was allowed under the Missouri Compromise.

authority over affairs in the Western Hemisphere (*see* **George Canning**). He declared that "the American continents . . . are henceforth not to be considered as subjects for future colonization by any European power." Any European interference in the former Spanish colonies in the New World would be regarded "as the manifestation of an unfriendly disposition toward the United States." He also added that America would not interfere with the existing colonies of any European power in the hemisphere and would never take part in European internal affairs or wars. Monroe's message —many portions of which were the work of **John Quincy Adams** (*see*)—was prompted by several developments. In 1821, Russia had extended her claims in the Pacific Northwest to include present-day Oregon and had banned all commercial shipping from coastal waters in the area. In addition, rumors had been circulating that a number of European nations were planning to reconquer Spain's former colonies in Latin America (*see pp. 368–369*). The rumors eventually proved false, but not because of anything Monroe said. His remarks were largely ignored until 1845, when President James K. Polk (1795–1849) repeated Monroe's principles in response to diplomatic maneuvers by Britain and France in North America. However, it was not until the 1850s that these principles were referred to as the Monroe Doctrine. During the Civil War, the doctrine was· invoked to condemn Spanish intervention in the Dominican Republic and also a French attempt to set up a puppet government in Mexico. Citing the Monroe Doctrine, American diplomats pressured both nations to withdraw from Latin America.

Since the 1870s, the doctrine has been cited with increasing frequency, and its interpretation has been expanded.

MORSE, Samuel F. B. (1791–1872). Morse pioneered the development of the electric telegraph, which revolutionized long-distance communication. Morse was born in Charlestown, Massachusetts. His father was the Reverend Jedidiah Morse (1761–1826), who wrote the first geography published in the United States (1784). After graduating from Yale in 1810, Morse studied painting in London. He returned to the United States in 1815 and later became a portrait painter in Charleston, South Carolina, and in New York City (*see pp. 375 and 444*). In 1825, Morse helped to found the National Academy of Design and was its first president (1826–1842). Although talented, he never achieved financial success as a painter. In 1832, he learned that the French physicist André Ampere (1775–1836) had conceived the idea of transmitting messages electrically. For the next

Samuel F. B. Morse

12 years, Morse worked on devising a practical telegraphic apparatus and a suitable electric "alphabet" (later known as Morse code) to transmit messages. He successfully demonstrated his invention to Congress on May 24, 1844. His first message, transmitted from Washington, D.C., to Baltimore, was, "What hath God wrought!" The commercial value of the telegraph was soon evident, and by the time of his death Morse was famous and wealthy.

N

NEAGLE, John (1796–1865). A portrait painter, Neagle was apprenticed as a youth to a "coach and ornamental" painter for more than five years. He set up a studio in Philadelphia and became a successful artist. His reputation was enhanced in 1826 by his portrait of Pat Lyon, a local blacksmith falsely accused of bank robbery. On a visit to Boston, Neagle painted a portrait of Gilbert Stuart (1755–1828) that is considered the finest likeness of that artist. It now hangs in the Boston Museum of Fine Arts. Neagle's portrait of George Washington (1732–1799) is in Independence Hall, Philadelphia, and his life-size picture of **Henry Clay** (*see*) hangs in the nation's Capitol (*see p. 395*).

O

ORDINANCE OF NULLIFICATION. South Carolinians were particularly bitter about the **Tariff of 1828** (*see*). Southern planters were forced to pay a high price to Northern manufacturers for products they could have bought more cheaply from Britain. In 1828, **John C. Calhoun** (*see*) argued that the federal government was favoring one section of the nation over another. He contended, in an anonymously written pamphlet, that every state had the right to nullify a federal law that it considered unconstitutional. In 1832, when a new bill passed by Congress did not substantially lower tariffs, the South Carolina legislature summoned a state convention. It adopted the Ordinance of Nullification in November, 1832. The ordinance declared the Tariffs of 1828 and 1832 null and void. Collection of the federal tariffs in South Carolina was to stop on February 1, 1833, and any attempt by the federal government to enforce the tariff would result in secession. President **Andrew Jackson** (*see*) responded by denouncing nullification as treason. He warned South Carolina that he would use force to execute the laws of the United States and asked Congress for this authority (*see* **Force Bill**). As a compromise, **Henry Clay** (*see*) proposed a reduction in tariffs, and the new tariff law became known as the **Compromise of 1833** (*see*).

P

PALMER, Nathaniel (1799–1877). A sea captain and explorer, "Captain Nat" discovered the mainland of Antarctica in 1820. A native of Stonington, Connecticut, Palmer first went to sea at the age of 14, sailing the coast between New York and Maine. On November 18, 1820, while searching the South Atlantic for new seal rookeries, the 21-year-old shipmaster discovered the Antarctic Continent, where an archipelago is now named after him. The following year he again explored the same region and discovered the

South Orkney Islands. In the 1830s, Palmer became a packet captain, sailing from New York to New Orleans and later to Liverpool. When trade with the Orient flourished, he took command of several fast China clipper ships, including the *Houqua, Oriental,* and *Samuel Russell.* In addition to sailing the clippers, Palmer suggested improvements in their design. In later life, he became a director of a steamship company.

PANIC OF 1819. The first serious economic crisis in the United States occurred in 1819. In the years following the War of 1812, many persons borrowed heavily to buy land on the Western frontier. State banks made it easy to obtain loans, and the **Second Bank of the United States** (*see*) contributed to the feverish borrowing by illegally printing currency that totaled more than 10 times the amount of the specie (gold and silver) behind it. Much of the booming American prosperity at this time was due to the large volume of farm produce being sold to European nations. However, when the Napoleonic Wars ended in 1815 and European food production revived, American exports dropped off rapidly. Suddenly, hard times struck. With no market, crops rotted in the fields and land values fell. Americans tried to turn in their paper money for "hard" money, but the banks did not have enough gold and silver to distribute. Businesses and banks failed, and unemployment rose. The ensuing depression lasted until 1822. Although not so serious as the **Panic of 1837** (*see*), the financial crisis of 1819 caused great suffering, especially in the West and South. The property of many people was sold to pay taxes or meet debts.

PANIC OF 1837. Many conditions and events contributed to the unsound economy that brought on the financial disaster of 1837. Among the causes were (1) huge state debts from the building of **canals** and **railroads** (*see both*), (2) the failure of exports to keep pace with imports, (3) poor crops, and (4) the lack of a sound federal Treasury system. Like the **Panic of 1819** (*see*), this crisis stemmed largely from the overextension of credit to purchase public lands. Between 1832 and 1836, annual receipts from the sale of federal lands increased almost tenfold. In New York City, nearly eight house lots had been sold for every resident. At Chicago, then only a village of less than 3,000 people, residential lots had been sold for 25 miles around. Farmers mortgaged their land to buy more land. Banks issued credit and paper money to keep pace with the booming demand, but the currency was backed by very little specie (gold and silver). In July of 1836, President **Andrew Jackson** (*see*) tried to end the wild speculation by issuing the **Specie Circular** (*see*), which declared that only gold or silver would be accepted for federal land. However, there was little specie available—and that was quickly hoarded. The land boom suddenly collapsed, and with it public confidence in the economy. Land and commodity prices plunged. Bankruptcies multiplied. In the spring of 1837, every bank in the nation closed. The unemployed rioted in New York. The nation entered a depression that lasted for six years.

PEABODY, George (1795–1869). A merchant and financier by profession, Peabody was one of the nation's leading philanthropists in

George Peabody

the 19th century. Born in South Danvers (now Peabody), Massachusetts, Peabody rose from a grocer's apprentice to become the senior partner of Riggs & Peabody, a Baltimore dry-goods firm, in 1829. In 1835, Peabody obtained an $8,000,000 British loan for the state of Maryland, which was nearly bankrupt, and refused any commission for his negotiations. Two years later, he settled in London, where he had established the brokerage firm of George Peabody & Company. During the next few years, when American foreign credit was weak because of the **Panic of 1837** (*see*), Peabody used his personal credit and influence to restore confidence in the American economy. He financed the display of American products at the 1851 Crystal Palace exhibition in England. Peabody founded and endowed the Peabody Institutes in Baltimore and Peabody, Massachusetts, the Peabody Museums at Yale and Harvard Universities, and the Peabody Education Fund to promote education in the South.

PHYFE, Duncan (1768–1854). This renowned furniture designer and manufacturer wielded a powerful influence on American taste in the early 1800s. After emigrating from Scotland about 1784, Phyfe was apprenticed to a cabinetmaker in Albany, New York. He set up his own shop in New York City in the early 1790s, and soon his business became so prosperous that he had 100 employees. Phyfe's chairs, tables, and sofas —adapted from designs by master craftsmen in England—were noted for their graceful proportions, simplicity, and fine detail. His fame rests on the furniture he produced before 1825. About that time, he gradually gave in to the popular demand for the so-called American Empire style. By the latter part of his career (1830–1847), Phyfe was designing cumbersome, grotesquely ornate forms, which became known as butcher furniture.

An 1837 Duncan Phyfe chair

POLITICAL PARTIES. The Constitution did not provide for political parties—in fact, many of the Founding Fathers feared that political parties would disrupt national unity. However, men of opposing interests and points of view soon began to create organizations to contest for governmental power. The Federalists, led by Alexander Hamilton (1755–1804), became the first American party soon after 1789. Favoring a strong central government presided over by wealthy property owners, they drew support mainly from commercial and industrial elements in the Northern states. Agricultural and rural interests, especially in the South, soon rallied around Thomas Jefferson (1743–1826) to found the Democratic-Republican Party about 1794. Although the Federalists controlled national policy in the early years of the nation, the Democrats—as Jefferson's Democratic-Republicans came to be known after 1828— dominated the government from 1800 until 1840. The Federalist Party, meanwhile, withered away, nominating its last Presidential candidate in 1816. Opponents of the Democrats joined together in 1836 to form the Whig Party, which won the Presidential elections of 1840 and 1848. The present Republican Party, created by a coalition of antislavery Whigs and other opponents of slavery, came into being in 1854. The Republicans elected Abraham Lincoln (1809–1865) in 1860 and held power continuously until 1884. Although the two-party system has been the rule ever since, several third parties were influential in early American politics. The Anti-Masonic Party, organized in 1826 to oppose secret societies, was absorbed by the Whigs about 1838. The Free Soil Party was chiefly interested in getting free land grants for settlers, but its members also opposed slavery. It and the antislavery Liberty Party

Whigs sought the votes of American industry in the election of 1844.

merged about 1848 and later became part of the Republican Party. The secretive American Party—often called the Know-Nothing Party because its members claimed ignorance of its activities—opposed immigration and Catholicism. It gained a substantial following during the 1850s but disbanded by 1860.

PORTER, Peter Buell (1773–1844). Porter, a Representative from New York (1809–1813), was a leader of the "war-hawk" faction in Congress before the War of 1812. A native of Connecticut, he graduated from Yale in 1791 and moved to upstate New York, where he became a lawyer and was instrumental in developing the city of Buffalo. Elected to Congress in 1809, he encouraged the government's construction of roads and canals and advocated the military conquest of Canada. After service as a major general in the War of 1812, Porter was again elected to the House of Representatives in 1815. After one term, he became a member of a special commission to settle the eastern boundary between the United States and Canada. With the

backing of **Henry Clay** (*see*), Porter was appointed Secretary of War in 1828. The following year, he retired from government.

R

RAILROADS. Railroads were one of the most important factors in the development of commerce, industry, and agriculture in the United States (*see pp. 435–441*). They were also responsible for the rapid settlement of the West. Railroads came into general use soon after 1830, when **Peter Cooper** (*see*) demonstrated with his tiny locomotive, *Tom Thumb,* that steam-powered transportation by land was practical. Before this time, cars on rails—drawn by horses or operated by cables— had been employed only in mining operations. Because of their speed and ability to function in all kinds of weather, railroads soon became the preferred means of transporting freight and passengers. Among the earliest American companies were the Baltimore & Ohio Railroad and the South Carolina Railroad, both of which began operations in 1830. Although the first railroads were designed for limited service between neighboring towns, small lines were soon joined to form giant networks such as the New York Central Railroad, organized in 1853. By 1840, there were nearly 3,000 miles of track in service. Twenty years later the total was 30,000 miles of track. At first, the cars traveled on wooden rails covered with straps of iron. These were replaced by heavy cast-iron rails in the 1840s and by steel rails in the 1860s. The Atlantic coast was linked to the Great Lakes by rail in 1851, and the first transcontinental railroad, a joint effort of the Union Pacific

and the Central Pacific, was completed in 1869. In the 1850s, coal-burning engines started to replace wood burners, and the advent of the telegraph permitted efficient dispatching of trains. In the following decade, track gauge (width), which varied from line to line, became increasingly standardized. Government subsidies in the form of land grants and tax benefits encouraged the growth of railroads but also led to corruption and monopoly. Overexpansion in railroad building contributed to the **Panic of 1837** (*see*). Wild speculation in railroad stocks and violent strikes by railroad employees after 1870 led to federal regulation of the lines. Northern railroad superiority during the Civil War played an important part in the Union victory. Although the railroads have declined somewhat in the 20th century because of strong competition from motor vehicles and airplanes, they are still a central element in America's transportation system.

RANDOLPH, John (1773–1833). Although he suffered most of his life from physical and mental ill-

John Randolph

nesses, Randolph was one of the most effective debaters in the House of Representatives. He represented Virginia for 24 years, between 1799 and 1829. Claiming to be a descendant of Pocahontas (1595?–1617), Randolph considered himself a born aristocrat. "I love liberty," he was fond of saying, "I hate equality." Most of his speeches in Congress consisted of violent attacks on policies with which he did not agree. Throughout his career, Randolph was against the Federalists and their efforts to set up a strong central government. He used his brilliant mind and bitter wit to champion individual liberty and states' rights. "Asking one of the States to surrender part of her sovereignty," he once announced, "is like asking a lady to surrender part of her chastity." He interpreted the Constitution strictly and disapproved of compromise even for political motives. After 1805, he attacked President Thomas Jefferson (1743–1826) and his administration. Randolph subsequently opposed, among other things, the War of 1812 against Britain, the establishment of the **Second Bank of the United States** (*see*) in 1816, and the **Missouri Compromise** (*see*). Randolph's denunciation of **Henry Clay** (*see*) led to a famous but bloodless pistol duel between the two men on April 8, 1826. Clay pierced Randolph's coat, but Randolph purposely fired into the air. While serving in the Senate (1825–1827), Randolph suffered one of his periodic attacks of mental illness and thereafter refrained from speaking. He later served briefly as the American minister to Russia in 1830 but resigned because of his health. His last years were ruined by heavy drinking and mental disorders.

RUSH, Richard (1780–1859). Rush, a diplomat and statesman who was the acting Secretary of State in 1817, negotiated the **Rush-Bagot Agreement** (*see*) with the British minister, **Sir Charles Bagot** (*see*). This treaty limited American and British naval armament on the Great Lakes. Born in Philadelphia, Rush became a lawyer in 1800. He was the attorney general of Pennsylvania and Comptroller of the United States before serving (1814–1817) as Attorney General of the United States. In 1817, Rush served briefly as Secretary of State until **John Quincy Adams** (*see*) returned from Europe to assume that position. As minister to Britain (1817–1825), Rush was influential in the development of the **Monroe Doctrine** (*see*). He was Secretary of the Treasury (1825–1828) under Adams and ran as the Vice-Presidential candidate in Adams' unsuccessful bid for reelection in 1828. Rush returned to England in 1836 to convert into cash an estate left to the United States by British chemist James Smithson (1765–1829). This generous legacy was used to establish the Smithsonian Institution in Washington, D.C., in 1846. Rush later served as minister to France (1847–1849).

RUSH–BAGOT AGREEMENT. The Rush-Bagot Agreement (or Convention) provided for American and British disarmament on the Great Lakes. It consisted of an exchange of notes between the British minister to the United States, **Sir Charles Bagot** (*see*), and the acting Secretary of State, **Richard Rush** (*see*), on April 28 and 29, 1817. The United States and Britain had fought many naval battles on the Great Lakes during the War of 1812, and after the end of hostilities, both gov-

ernments realized that the only way to prevent a race for naval superiority in those waters would be to limit naval armament. The Rush-Bagot Agreement stipulated that each nation could have one vessel on Lake Champlain, one on Lake Ontario, and two vessels each on Lakes Erie, Huron, Michigan, and Superior. None of these vessels could exceed 100 tons or carry more than one 18-pound cannon. The agreement was approved by the United States Senate on April 16, 1818 and remained in effect for many years. It was reaffirmed by the United States and Canada in 1946.

RUTGERS, Henry (1745–1830). Rutgers was a wealthy New York landowner who contributed generously to religious and educational institutions. In 1825, Queen's College in New Brunswick, New Jersey, of which he had been a trustee (1816–1821), changed its name to Rutgers College (now Rutgers—the State University) in his honor. Born in New York, Rutgers was an officer in the Revolution and later commanded a New York militia regiment until 1795. Rutgers was also a trustee (1804–1817) of the College of New Jersey (now Princeton University). From 1828 until his death, he was president of New York's Free School Society.

S

SAINT-AULAIRE, Felix Achille (1801–?). Saint-Aulaire was a French landscapist and lithographer who visited the United States in 1821. He traveled as far west as the Ohio River. On the north bank of that river, across from Guyandotte, in present-day West Virginia, he painted a watercolor (*see pp. 412–413*) that is one of the earliest-known depictions of a keelboat and a flatboat. (Saint-Aulaire portrayed himself working in the foreground.) In 1832, after he had returned to France, he produced several lithographs of American scenes.

SECOND BANK OF THE UNITED STATES.

Incorporated by an act of Congress in 1816, this bank was created to restore financial order in the nation after the War of 1812. Modeled after its predecessor, the First Bank of the United States, whose charter had lapsed in 1811, the new bank was designed to provide the nation with a central banking system and to handle the monetary transactions of the federal government. The charter capitalized the bank at $35,000,000 and authorized it to issue notes equal to that amount. The government was obligated to supply one-fifth of the capital, and the President was empowered to select five of the 25-man board of directors. The remaining directors were elected by the private shareholders. In its first years, the bank suffered from mismanagement, but when **Nicholas Biddle** (*see*) took over in 1823, it prospered. The bank was centered in Philadelphia, with 25 branches throughout the states. The bank helped curb inflationary tendencies and was a factor in the nation's overall economic well-being. However, opposition developed from state banks, whose policies of easy credit were restricted by the more conservative national bank, and from small businessmen in the South and West, who viewed it as benefiting only Eastern commerce. One of the most vocal opponents was President **Andrew Jackson** (*see*), who regarded the bank as a

"hydra of corruption." Aware of Jackson's antagonism, Biddle applied to Congress for a new charter in 1831, five years before the actual expiration date. Jackson vetoed the bill, and the bank became the main issue of his successful campaign for reelection in 1832. Jackson interpreted his victory as a popular mandate to destroy the bank. In 1833, he withdrew its federal funds and deposited them in state banks, which became known as pet banks. When the bank's charter ran out in 1836, Biddle continued it as a private institution under the name of the Bank of the United States of Pennsylvania. This bank operated until it was forced to liquidate in 1841.

SEMINOLES.

After two bitter and costly wars with the United States Army between 1816 and 1842, the Seminoles were forced to migrate to present-day Oklahoma. A few escaped into the Florida Everglades. The Seminole tribe was formed during the 18th century by Creeks who moved from present-day Alabama to

Spanish Florida and united with members of other tribes, including the Apalachees, Yuchis, and Yamasees. The Creek word *seminole* means "separatist" or "fugitive." The Seminoles' capacity to absorb diverse peoples, including runaway Negro slaves, brought on the first Seminole War (1816–1818). **Andrew Jackson** (*see*), instructed to recover the renegade slaves and to punish the Indians for raids on settlers, successfully subdued the Seminoles in 1818 (*see* **Arbuthnot-Ambrister Affair**). By the Treaty of Payne's Landing in 1832, the Seminoles were to be relocated west of the Mississippi. However, led by Osceola (1800?–1838), many of them repudiated the treaty and went to war again in 1835. The Seminoles were finally crushed in 1842, at the cost of about 1,500 American lives and about $30,000,000. In Oklahoma, the Seminoles joined the Cherokee, Chickasaw, Choctaw, and Creek nations in forming the Five Civilized Tribes in 1859. In the 1980 census, there were less than 2,000 Seminoles still remaining in Southern Florida.

This 1837 print, published in Charleston, South Carolina, shows Seminoles attacking a blockhouse in Florida during their second war against settlers.

Sequoyah with his syllabary

SEQUOYAH (1770?–1843). The man who devised a syllabary (table of syllables) for the **Cherokees** (*see*) was the son of a white trader and a Cherokee woman. Raised as an Indian, Sequoyah grew up ignorant of English and lived as a hunter and fur trader until he was crippled by an accident. He then turned to making silver ornaments. He came into increased contact with white traders and became fascinated with their written language, which he called "talking leaves." In 1809, Sequoyah began to analyze his own language and by 1821 had produced a table of 86 characters representing groups of sounds in the Cherokee tongue. His first successful pupil was his six-year-old daughter. That same year, the Cherokee council of chiefs approved the syllabary, and soon thousands of Cherokees had learned to read and write. Sequoyah later moved with the Cherokees when they were forced to settle in Oklahoma. He died in 1843 while searching for a legendary Cherokee tribe in Mexico. The giant sequoia redwoods of California and Sequoia National Park in that state are named in his honor.

SINGER, Isaac Merritt (1811–1875). Singer's name has become a household word throughout the world because of the sewing machine he designed, which still bears his name. Singer was born in Pittstown, New York. His first two inventions—a rock-drilling machine (1839) and a wood-and-metal-carving machine (1849)—met with little success. In 1851, he built the first practical sewing machine for home use. Although it was partly based on a model patented by **Elias Howe** (*see*), Singer's machine was better and more versatile because it could do continuous and curved stitching. Later that year, Singer founded I. M. Singer & Company and continued to perfect his machine. During the next 12 years, he patented 20 improvements on his original machine. Nevertheless, because Howe's machine was declared by the court to be the basic invention, Singer had to pay Howe

The original Singer sewing machine of 1851 had to be cranked by hand.

royalties on each machine that he sold. Singer later merged with Howe, as well as with other competitors, and became the leading sewing-machine manufacturer in America. In 1863, he retired and went to live in Europe. The inventor died in Devonshire, England, on July 23, 1875.

SLATER, Samuel (1768–1835). Slater founded the cotton-spinning industry in America (*see pp. 380–381*). Born in Derbyshire, England, Slater was apprenticed as a youth to an associate of Richard Arkwright (1732–1792), who had invented water-driven machinery for producing cotton yarn. During the six years of his apprenticeship, Slater became familiar with the construction of the complicated textile machinery. At this time, the designs for this valuable equipment were a closely guarded secret. The British government prohibited anyone from taking the plans or equipment out of the country and did not allow textile workers to emigrate. Slater, however, determined to go to America, where bonuses were being paid for workers skilled in textiles. In disguise, he sailed for America in 1789. The next year, he met **Moses Brown** (*see*) and joined his company. Their first factory was opened in Pawtucket, Rhode Island, with machines Slater built from memory. He later expanded his cotton-milling operations to Connecticut, Massachusetts, and New Hampshire.

SMITH, Margaret Bayard (1778–1844). Mrs. Smith, the wife of a well-known Democratic-Republican editor, left a long, detailed record of social and political life in Washington, D.C., during the early years of the nation. A collection of her letters, entitled *The First Forty Years of Washington Society,* was published posthumously in 1906. Although her husband, Samuel H. Smith (1772–1845), was an ardent Jeffersonian, Mrs. Smith was a Federalist. Hence, leaders of both major political parties were frequently invited to their home. In addition to her social activities in the capital, Mrs. Smith wrote novels and contributed articles to various literary periodicals.

SPECIE CIRCULAR. The Specie Circular was designed to curb inflation and land speculation by requiring gold and silver (specie) for the purchase of public lands. The expanded use of paper currency and the easy credit provided by the banks between 1832 and 1836 had multiplied land sales in the West almost tenfold. This, combined with the removal of federal funds from the **Second Bank of the United States** (*see*) in 1833 by President **Andrew Jackson** (*see*), left the nation on the brink of financial chaos. To restore order, Senator **Thomas Hart Benton** (*see*) drafted for Jackson the Specie Circular, which eliminated the use of bank notes as payment for government land, thus making gold and silver the only acceptable form of money in circulation. Although the Specie Circular discouraged land speculation and strengthened Western banks, it also depleted reserves of gold and silver in Eastern banks, led to hoarding of these precious metals, diminished public confidence in state banks, and hastened the **Panic of 1837** (*see*). In that year, Congress passed a bill revoking the circular, but Jackson vetoed it. The circular was finally abolished by a joint resolution of Congress in 1838.

SPOILS SYSTEM. The time-honored practice of rewarding political supporters with jobs in governmental posts has become known in the United States as the spoils system. The phrase originated in 1832, after Senator William L. Marcy (1786–1857) of New York declared in Congress, "to the victor belong the spoils"

—that is, the booty captured in war. Although every previous President had appointed some supporters to office, it was **Andrew Jackson** (*see*) who first made widespread use of the practice. During his eight years in office (1829–1837), Jackson replaced about 20% of the federal officeholders with Democratic appointees, defending his action as a healthy "rotation" of personnel. When Jackson's opponents came to power after 1840, they replaced his appointees with their own followers. The most notorious use of the spoils system occurred during the administration (1869–1877) of Ulysses S. Grant (1822–1885), when many important federal offices became payoffs for unqualified party hacks. Public clamor for reform following the assassination of James A. Garfield (1831–1881) by a disappointed office seeker finally led to the Pendleton Act of 1883, which created the modern civil service. This placed many public posts under a merit system, with qualifications for office determined by competitive examinations. However, there are still many jobs, both federal and state, filled by appointment.

STEAMBOATS. Although British and French inventors were toying with the possibility of steam-powered boats as early as the 17th century, it was not until John Fitch (1743–1798) launched the first American steamboat on the Delaware River in 1787 that such experiments became practical. James Rumsey (1743–1792) launched a steamboat on the Potomac River the same year, but the *Clermont,* built by Robert Fulton (1765–1815), marked the beginning of practical commercial steam navigation with her voyage up the Hudson from New York to

Albany in 1807 (*see pp. 382–383*). The first steamboat on Western waters was the *New Orleans* (1811), a 300-ton, two-masted side-wheeler, which sailed up the Mississippi to Natchez. This was the model steamboat until 1816, when Henry Shreve (1785–1851) built the *Washington,* a double-deck side-wheeler with a low hull. Her success assured the future of steam navigation on shallow Western waters. Within 30 years, more than 1,000 steamboats were running, carrying freight and passengers on the Mississippi, Missouri, Tennessee, Ohio, and Illinois Rivers. Pittsburgh, Louisville, and Cincinnati became the great Ohio ports, and New Orleans and St. Louis ranked high in steam tonnage in America (*see pp. 412–419*). Corporations were formed to handle the river traffic, among them the Cincinnati and Louisville Mail Line, the Northern Line, and the Anchor Line. As traffic increased, the design of steamboats improved. Many of the boats became floating hotels, with elaborately decorated cabins, private staterooms, shops, bars, wide decks, and promenades. By 1860, steam-operated vessels were carrying over 10,000,000 tons of freight each year and maintaining regularly scheduled overseas passenger services, including a New York to Liverpool run.

T

TALLMADGE, James (1778–1853). As a Representative (1817–1819) from New York, Tallmadge introduced in the House in 1819 the amendment that began the controversy over Missouri's admission to the Union. It was designed to prohibit the further introduction of slaves into the proposed new state. It further stipulated that all slaves born in Missouri after it gained statehood would be freed at the age of 25. The ensuing controversy was resolved by the **Missouri Compromise** (*see*). Tallmadge later served as lieutenant governor of New York (1825–1827) and shortly thereafter retired from politics. He was a founder of the University of the City of New York (now New York University).

TANEY, Roger (1777–1864). Taney, who succeeded **John Marshall** (*see*) as Chief Justice of the Supreme Court in 1835, favored states' rights over the authority of the federal government. The son of a Maryland slave owner, Taney became a lawyer and by the early 1800s was a leader of the Federalist Party. Taney eventually joined the Democrats and in 1831 was appointed Attorney General by President **Andrew Jackson** (*see*). Convinced that the **Second Bank of the United States** (*see*) was too powerful, Taney helped persuade Jackson to veto the rechartering of the bank. He also urged Jackson to remove government deposits from the bank and place them in state banks. He was named Secretary of the Treasury in 1833 to supervise the undertaking, but the Senate refused to ratify his appointment and two years later would not confirm his nomination as Associate Justice of the Supreme Court. After Marshall's death in 1835, the Senate reversed itself and consented to Taney's filling the vacancy. He served for 28 years (1836–1864). Unlike Marshall, who had advocated a strong central government, Taney gave the states as much sovereignty as possible. He gradually came to defend the

Roger Taney

Southern states against the federal government, which he believed was increasingly dominated by Northern interests. Although he freed his own slaves, Taney viewed slavery as a necessary evil and upheld slavery laws. In the Dred Scott case of 1857, Taney ruled that Scott was a slave and, as such, was not entitled to sue in the federal courts. This decision touched off a furor among abolitionists and Republicans and helped lead to the Civil War.

TARIFF OF ABOMINATIONS. *See* **Tariff of 1828.**

TARIFF OF 1828. This protective tariff sparked a controversy that almost resulted in the secession of South Carolina from the Union. The first protective tariff in the nation was passed in 1816 and was designed to encourage the development of domestic industries. However, the South did not succeed in developing industries on a large scale and became resentful when a further increase in tariffs was made in 1824. Four years later, supporters of Presidential candidate **Andrew Jackson** (*see*) attempted a political maneuver that backfired. They launched a campaign for a protective tariff

so high that it would not stand a chance of getting through Congress. The idea was that Northern Congressmen would object to the excessive duties on raw materials for Northern industries and that their votes, combined with those of the South, would defeat the tariff. Thus, in the national election that fall, Jackson would supposedly win support in the North for having favored in principle a high tariff, and support in the South for defeating it. However, several New England Senators decided to back the tariff measure because it protected the woolen industry in their area. The tariff was passed and soon became known among its enemies as the Tariff of Abominations. **John C. Calhoun** (*see*) anonymously published a pamphlet favoring nullification of the tariff by the states themselves, which in 1832 prompted South Carolina to adopt the **Ordinance of Nullification** (*see*).

THOMAS, Jesse (1777–1853). A Senator (1818–1829) from Illinois, Thomas introduced the amendment that convinced many Senators from free states to vote for the **Missouri Compromise** (*see*) in 1820. Although he supported slavery, Thomas proposed to prohibit it in the Louisiana Territory north of 36° 30′ latitude—a line running along Missouri's southern boundary. This plan became part of the compromise that was finally enacted. Earlier, Thomas was speaker (1805–1808) of the Indiana territorial legislature and worked for the independent status of Illinois, which was then part of Indiana. When Illinois achieved statehood in 1818, Thomas became one of its first two Senators. Afterward, he moved to Ohio, where he prospered in business.

THURBER, Charles (1803–1886). In 1843, Thurber was granted a patent for a hand printing machine, the forerunner of the modern typewriter. It incorporated a moving carriage and a method of turning paper after a line was completed. However, no one seemed interested in the machine's commercial possibilities, and it was not manufactured. Thurber was born in Massachusetts. After graduating from Brown University in 1827, he taught school for several years before going into business in 1836 as a firearms manufacturer in Worcester. Before he retired in 1856, he also devised a machine to aid the blind in writing.

TOCQUEVILLE, Alexis de (1805–1859). Tocqueville's *Democracy in America,* published in 1835, is regarded as one of the most brilliant commentaries ever written on American political and social systems. Tocqueville was born in Verneuil, France. He completed studies for the bar in 1826 and became an assistant magistrate. Sent to study American prisons in 1831, he traveled over much of the United States during the next two years. His study of the American

Alexis de Tocqueville

penal system, written with Gustave de Beaumont (1802–1866), was published in 1833 in France. Tocqueville then devoted himself to writing his classic study of American democracy. Translated into the major European languages, the book won him international fame and election to the French Academy in 1841. Although praising the freedoms contained in the American system, Tocqueville issued his famous warning against the "tyranny of the majority," which he said could deprive minority groups of their rights. Tocqueville showed a great understanding of the American character and was startlingly accurate in foretelling the course of economic and political developments in the United States. In 1848, Tocqueville became a member of the Chamber of Deputies and a year later was made French foreign minister. In 1851, he was forced out of office when Louis Napoleon (1808–1873) seized control of the government.

TRAIL OF TEARS. *See* **Cherokees.**

TWELFTH AMENDMENT. The Twelfth Amendment to the Constitution gave recognition to the party system by stipulating that members of the electoral college are to vote separately for the President and the Vice-President. Until this amendment was ratified in September, 1804, each elector simply cast two votes. The candidate receiving the greatest number became President, while the candidate receiving the second-highest number became Vice-President. The disadvantages of the old procedure became apparent in the election of 1800, when Thomas Jefferson (1743–1826) and Aaron Burr (1756–1836), both Demo-

cratic-Republicans, received the same number of electoral votes. Jefferson and Burr had run with the intention of becoming President and Vice-President, respectively. However, under the Constitution, the electors had been unable to specify which man was to get which office. Thus, according to the Constitution, the election had to be decided in the House of Representatives. After a bitter struggle, Jefferson became President, and Burr, Vice-President. The Twelfth Amendment was adopted to prevent this situation from recurring by having the electors vote for separate lists of candidates for the two offices. It also declared that, lacking a majority in the electoral vote, the President was to be chosen by the House from the three candidates receiving the highest number of votes. The Vice-President was to be chosen by the Senate from the two leading candidates. This amendment was invoked in 1825 when the House elected **John Quincy Adams** over **William H. Crawford** and **Andrew Jackson** (*see all*), and in 1837, when the Senate selected **Richard Johnson** (*see*).

V

VAN BUREN, Martin (1782–1862). The eighth President of the United States, Van Buren favored states' rights over strong federal authority. Born in Kinderhook, near Albany, New York, Van Buren was known both as the Red Fox of Kinderhook and the Little Magician because of his sharp political practices. He began practicing law in 1803 and also became involved in state and national election campaigns. He served as a state senator (1812–1820) and then as attorney general of New York (1815–1819). Van Buren—a Democrat and leader of an influential group of New York politicians that became known as the Albany Regency—represented New York in the United States Senate (1821–1828) before being elected governor in 1829. He resigned that post the same year to become Secretary of State (1829–1831) under **Andrew Jackson** (*see*). Van Buren was named minister to Britain in 1831, but Vice-President **John C. Calhoun** (*see*), a political rival, blocked his appointment in the Senate. With Jackson's support, Van Buren was elected Vice-President in 1832 and President four years later. Van Buren believed that individual states and communities should be responsible for solving their own problems. When the **Panic of 1837** (*see*) occurred, he opposed the use of federal funds to alleviate the depression that followed. "The less government interferes with private pursuits the better for the general prosperity," he declared. Van Buren's proposal for an independent Treasury, which removed federal money from state banks, provoked bitter protest from business interests. Although he was against slavery on principle, Van Buren's belief in states' rights led him to oppose federal action to abolish slavery in the South. He was defeated for reelection in 1840 and was again an unsuccessful candidate for President eight years later, this time on the antislavery Free Soil ticket. Van Buren then retired to his farm in upstate New York, where he died on July 24, 1862.

W

WEBSTER–HAYNE DEBATE.
In January, 1830, the philosophies of nationalism and states' rights were debated by Daniel Webster (1782–1852) of Massachusetts and **Robert Hayne** (*see*) of South Carolina in a series of speeches before the Senate. The debate was prompted by the introduction of a resolution to restrict the sale of public lands in the West. On January 19, 1830, Hayne rose to speak in opposition to the resolution and accused New England Congressmen of restricting development in the West. The following day, Webster denied Hayne's charges and accused him of having an indifferent attitude toward the Union. Angered by Webster's remarks, Hayne replied on January 25. For two-and-a-half hours, he discussed the disloyalty of the New England Federalists during the War of 1812, attacked protective tariffs, introduced the doctrine of nullification (*see* **Ordinance of Nullification**), and contended that the Constitution implied that the states had sovereignty over the federal government. Webster's emotional reply, delivered over the next two days, ran a total of more than four hours. He largely avoided the economic issues Hayne had raised. Instead, Webster focused on the meaning of the Constitution as a workable document, concluding, "Liberty *and* Union, now and forever, one and inseparable!" Hayne attempted a rebuttal the same day, but Webster's speech was published and distributed throughout the nation and is remembered as one of the most eloquent speeches ever delivered in defense of the federal Union.

WEEMS, Mason Locke (1759–1825).
Parson Weems is best remembered as the author of the legend about George Washington (1732–1799) and the cherry tree. An Episcopal minister, Weems preached in Maryland from 1784 to 1792. He entered the book trade, and convinced that he could spread the word of God to a wider audience, became an itinerant bookseller in 1794. For the next 31 years, he traveled up and down the Eastern coast, dispensing morally "uplifting" literature. He also wrote a number of biographies of noted persons, including *The Life and Memorable Actions of George Washington,* which became an immediate best seller in 1800. The cherry-tree myth, which

NEW YORK PUBLIC LIBRARY

Weems' story about Washington and the cherry tree inspired moral lessons.

established Washington as a moral example for American youth to follow, was included in the fifth edition of the book in 1806. According to Weems' story, Washington, when a young boy, chopped down a cherry tree in his father's orchard. When his father asked who had done it, George replied, "I can't tell a lie, Pa. . . . I did cut it with my hatchet."

WHITNEY, Eli (1765–1825). Whitney's two major contributions to technology—the cotton gin and interchangeable machine parts—revolutionized the American economy (*see pp. 442–448*). Born in Massachusetts, Whitney worked in his father's machine shop and taught school before entering Yale in 1789. Three years later, he went to Georgia to study law. While there, Whitney was asked to devise a way to separate cotton fibers from their seeds. As a result, in 1793 he built a labor-saving device called a cotton "gin" (short for *engine*). It enabled a man to clean 50 pounds of cotton a day. By 1800, Whitney's machine was in such widespread use that the South was able to increase its annual cotton exports from 150,000 pounds to 18,000,-000 pounds. Whitney, however, made little money with his invention because of a lawsuit over his patent rights. His other innovation, a system of interchangeable gun parts, was developed in 1798 when Whitney opened a firearms factory outside New Haven. There he reduced the complex process of manufacturing weapons to a few simple mechanical operations. As a result, even unskilled workmen could make gun parts of uniform quality. Whitney's technological principles were soon adopted throughout the United States. They became known as the Amer-ican system and eventually led to mass production.

WIRT, William (1772–1834). Wirt was the first Attorney General of the United States (1817–1829) to record his legal opinions so that they could serve as precedents for future Attorneys General. Among the important cases he argued before the Supreme Court were *McCulloch vs. Maryland* in 1819, and *Gibbons vs. Ogden* in 1824 (*see both*). Born in Maryland, Wirt moved to Virginia as a young man and became a lawyer there in 1791. His legal reputation was enhanced in 1807 when he was selected as one of the government prosecutors in the treason trial of Aaron Burr (1756–1836). Wirt was also an author. His most popular work was a series of essays called *The Letters of the British Spy* (1803). Supposedly written by a British traveler, the letters were sympathetic studies of American life. In 1832, Wirt was an unsuccessful candidate for the Presidency on the Anti-Masonic Party ticket (*see* **political parties**).

WORCESTER, Samuel Austin (1798–1859). A Congregational missionary to the **Cherokees** (*see*), Worcester was the central figure in a Supreme Court decision that invalidated the annexation of Indian territory by Georgia (*see Worcester vs. Georgia*). Worcester at the time was in prison for failing to take out a state license to live among the Indians. Despite the ruling by Chief Justice **John Marshall** (*see*) upholding the tribe's property claim in 1832, Georgia refused to obey the Court and was finally able to get federal support to force the Cherokees to leave the state. Born in Worcester, Massachusetts, a descendant of the town's founder, Worcester graduated from Andover Theological Seminary in 1823. From 1825 until his death, he worked among the Cherokees, teaching them to read and write their language and translating the Bible into Cherokee. He helped to establish the *Cherokee Phoenix,* a pioneer Indian newspaper.

WORCESTER VS. GEORGIA. This Supreme Court case was another example of the recurring controversy between the federal government and the states as to the scope of their respective powers. The **Cherokees** (*see*) had negotiated a treaty with the United States in 1827 to establish an independent nation in part of Georgia. Georgia settlers, however, refused to recognize the Indians' claim. Georgia then annexed the tribe's lands and passed a law forbidding white men to live in Cherokee territory without first signing a loyalty oath to Georgia and purchasing a state license. When **Samuel A. Worcester** (*see*) and other missionaries to the Cherokees refused to obey the Georgia law, they were convicted and sentenced to prison. Worcester appealed his conviction to the Supreme Court. In 1832, Chief Justice **John Marshall** (*see*) ruled in favor of Worcester and the Cherokees. He said that Georgia had no jurisdiction over the region rightfully belonging to the Cherokees because the tribe was under the protection of the federal government. Thus, Georgia's law requiring oaths of allegiance was unconstitutional. However, Marshall's decision did not change matters. Georgia would not comply with the verdict, and President **Andrew Jackson** (*see*) backed Georgia, reportedly stating, "John Marshall has made his decision, now let him enforce it."